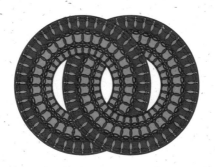

B of O D Y
DIMINISHING MOTION

POEMS AND A MEMOIR

B of ODY
DIMINISHING MOTION

POEMS AND A MEMOIR

Joan Seliger
Sidney

Joan Seliger Sidney

CavanKerry ❦ Press LTD.

Library of Congress Cataloging-in-Publication Data

Sidney, Joan Seliger, 1942–
Body of diminishing motion : poems and a memoir / by Joan Seliger
Sidney
Sidney. — 1st ed.
    p. cm.
Includes bibliographical references and index.
  ISBN 0-9723045-2-5
I. Multiple sclerosis—Patients—Poetry 2. Multiple
sclerosis—Patients—United States—Biography. 3. Poets. American—20th
century—Biography. 4. Sidney, Joan Seliger, 1942– 1. Title.
PS3569.I318B63 2004
811'.54–dc22
                                                        2003019429

Cover Art: *Hands* © 2004 by Maida Rosenheck
Author Photograph by Richard Telford
Cover and book design by Peter Cusack

First Edition
Printed in the United States of America

CavanKerry Press Ltd.
Fort Lee, New Jersey
www.cavankerrypress.org

LaurelBooks

Body of Diminishing Motion is the second title of CavanKerry's Literature of Illness imprint. *LaurelBooks* are fine collections of poetry and prose that explore the many poignant issues associated with confronting serious physical and/or psychological illness.

CavanKerry is grateful to the Arnold P. Gold Foundation for the Advancement of Humanism in Medicine for joining us in sponsoring this imprint. Offering *LaurelBooks* as teaching tools to medical schools is the result of shared concerns—humanism, community, and meeting the needs of the underserved. Together with the Gold Foundation, CavanKerry's two outreach efforts, *GiftBooks* and *Presenting Poetry & Prose*, will bring complimentary books and readings to the medical community at major hospitals across the United States.

The Arnold P. Gold Foundation

CavanKerry Press is grateful for the support it
receives from the New Jersey State Council on the Arts.

THE GREATEST LOVE

At fifty-eight, she no longer
questions: *What is grace?*

In her power-chair, she strolls
around the block, embracing
the edge of the chip-sealed street,
her dear one at her right,
his body both shield and flare.

At the pond they pause: November
light, two maples shimmering
naked across the surface.
Two sandpipers splash
fresh water on their wings.

In this 35th year of marriage
he takes her hand, kisses
each finger for the first time.

The problem . . . is how
to live in a damaged body
in a world where pain is meant to be gagged
uncured   un-grieved-over   The problem is
to connect, without hysteria, the pain
of any one's body with the pain of the body's world

— ADRIENNE RICH

CONTENTS

FOUR: HIKING REMOTE TRAILS

BEYOND MEDICINE AND DOCTORS: BUILDING A LIFE OVER CHRONIC ILLNESS

Multiple sclerosis, or MS, is well known but not well understood. It is a frightening neurological disease notorious for its unpredictable starts and stops, and for the variability of its symptoms and severity. MS can cause catastrophic blindness and paralysis over just a few days, or subtle and temporary sensory disturbances over a lifetime. It affects millions of people worldwide and, inexplicably, is much more common among those who grow up in colder climates, in places well away from the equator. Symptoms of MS typically first appear around the age of thirty and a majority of patients have further symptoms and acquire permanent problems with movement, sensation, and, sometimes, cognition, over the next fifteen to twenty years.

Because MS is a common and heartbreaking condition, it has been exhaustively studied. We know what the disease looks like under a microscope and in a brain scan, who is at risk of developing MS, and volumes more about its symptoms and diagnosis. We believe that immunological derangement, at least in part, contributes to the neurological dysfunction. And there have been exciting advances in how we manage our patients with the development of therapies that decrease the likelihood of future MS attacks. But MS has frustrated all efforts to answer two crucial questions: what causes it and how can it be cured? Consequently, the incidence of the disease is the same today as it was a hundred years ago, and once the diagnosis is made, more symptoms and variable degrees of neurological impairment are expected. On the bright side, the odds of discovering what causes MS and devising ways to prevent it or ameliorate its symptoms are increasingly in our favor.

So those are the facts about MS. But what is it like to have this chronic condition? This question is of great importance because it informs us about quality-of-life issues that must be appreciated by physicians and other care-givers, as well as family and friends. Once MS asserts itself, the idea of a "normal" life is continuously challenged by the burden of neurological impairments. How does one rebuild a satisfying everyday existence in the face of a disease that is so famously fickle? How does one continue to build all of the human relationships that give life its deepest and most important meaning?

Joan Sidney has MS and has confronted the gamut of practical and interpersonal dilemmas that can ensue. In this collection of her writings, she helps us experience her personal contest with this harsh illness. It is profoundly true that each person with MS has a unique story. It is equally true that there are shadowy common themes and Sidney's voice skillfully illuminates many of these. Yes, this is a collection that will resonate most strongly with those who are familiar with MS or have lived with chronic illnesses, but the real beauty is that she has created satisfying literature that can be enjoyed on its own merits.

Sidney's portrait of life with MS is fresh and sensitive, and very much needed. Wielding her art in a brave and unflinching way, she provides a wonderfully nuanced and emotionally true account of living with an unpredictable but relentless enemy bent on sabotaging communication within her brain. Her poetry and prose touch only lightly on the medical aspects of MS. Neurologists and textbooks, and even the Internet, are available to address those issues. She is our correspondent on the front lines of this disease, and her reports, some of them anguished, tell of humbling losses, unexpected family dilemmas and victories in the pursuit of personal goals. The triumph of this body of work is its subliminal message: we can't presently vanquish MS but we need not be dominated by it.

It is a shortsighted notion and simply not true that physicians alone, however dedicated, can coach their MS patients to achieve the highest quality of life possible. Neurologists specializing in MS can provide specific advice about medications and symptom management. But there is so much more to living successfully with MS than taking the right medications. What lies beyond are countless choices and adjustments, mental and emotional, that will determine for each person with MS if he or she will continue to relish daily existence or rue it. Support groups within the MS community and the national MS organizations are excellent resources for advice and help. What we have lacked are authentic voices like Sidney's that add detail and emotional tone to life with a chronic illness. It is not enough to encourage those with debilitating illnesses to remain active and engaged with families and careers; they need to identify with others who are dealing daily with similar obstacles. It helps, of course, if your guide is a gifted writer who is unafraid to touch upon sensitive matters such as intimacy and self-fulfillment.

No life is untouched by illness. If we are lucky, our illnesses are brief and reversible. They gently remind us how good we normally feel and cause a twinge of guilt for taking our health for granted. We are not pre-pared for serious chronic illness and simply can't grasp its impact, espe-cially from an emotional perspective. Sidney's poetry and her essay elo-quently reveal this world. We return from the experience with insights and admiration.

— Bruce R. Ransom M.D., Ph.D.
Warren Magnuson Professor and Chair,
Department of Neurology
University of Washington
Seattle, Washington

MIRACLES WITH FLAWS

The Psalmist says, "I am fearfully and wonderfully made." And yet, as Sherwin Nuland understands in his book, *The Wisdom of the Body*, we are "of necessity, miracles with flaws." The body, despite the inexorable march of scientific and medical advances, remains pretty much what it was centuries ago: an inscrutable mystery. Those flaws that Nuland speaks of can remain hidden within the body for many years, almost imperceptibly making themselves felt, or they can burst forth all at once. One morning some thirty-five years ago, Joan Sidney tells us in the prose memoir that makes up section four of *Body of Diminishing Motion*, her knee buckled on the stairs of the high school where she was teaching. It would be ten years before her body made known the meaning of that incident—she had MS—and all the years since for her to learn a very difficult lesson: healing is not synonymous with being cured.

In these poems and memoir, Joan Sidney sets out to tackle two difficult, but related problems: "how to live in a damaged body / in a world where pain is meant to be gagged" and how to "connect without hysteria, the pain / of any one's body with the pain of the body's world" (see the epigraph for *Body of Diminishing Motion* from Adrienne Rich). The body must learn the difficult lessons of "diminishing motion"; the poet inside the body must come to grips with the diminishments of her family: a grandmother tossed in a pit in Zurawno; the murder of her father's brother and sisters in the Holocaust; the endlessly repeated survivors' tale of her own parents who saw what was happening before they fled. In her emotionally complex and rich initial poem, "Preserves," the poet lays down the interwoven themes of her book. The speaker and her mother are making blueberry preserves. As the mother recalls buying as many blueberries as possible from a wagon that came through Zurawno because the "season was so short, the winter so long," the speaker wonders how she can tell her mother, who has suffered so many losses, about her MS, about why she "drags her feet to walk." In both the past and present, what is being preserved is also what is being lost—the summer, Jewish life in Zurawno, the daughter speaker's promise and mobility.

Body of Diminishing Motion makes a rare conjunction between the personal and private and the public and communal. In the first of its three sections of poems, Joan Sidney braids the challah of her own nerve cells diseased by MS and the emotions and sufferings imprinted in her by genes which were tossed in a pit in Zurawno, worked and starved to death in Auschwitz. If healing is the ultimate goal, then the speaker must acknowledge in this opening section that healing begins in the hellish, shadowy past of her ancestors ("*Body of Diminishing Motion*"). The way to the light is through that darkness and, throughout this first section, the speaker learns to hold to the love that makes us human ("*Oysgevept*") despite sickness and death. These poems cultivate memories into speech because "we are closer/in our sorrow than we've ever been" ("Next Door"). The second section looks more directly at the speaker's MS—the poems contemplate what was, what is, and what is to come. The lost body of pleasures ("Nude" and "Jin Shin Do") wars with the present body in which cells are destroying each other. And yet, the speaker forces herself to acknowledge that the real "betrayal" is not simply her body, but the "dis-ease" of her own litany of complaints, frustrations, hatreds, and angers. To be healed, the speaker knows, if only intuitively, love must be set "in motion."

The third section of poems brings together the "damaged body" and the "pain of the body's world." To set healing "in motion" the speaker knows that she must accept the difference between her spirit's healing and the cure she has sought, but which will never be found, for her body's breakdown. She knows, too, that she must accept the paradox of the past—the way it is both a prison and a path to freedom. It is the past, and particularly the speaker's mother's past, that is suffocating—"How many have you dragged/into your Holocaust past?" the speaker asks her mother. In her mother's world there is no other town but Zurawno ("Leaving"). And yet to live again, the speaker must learn to "forge links" with this past without allowing it to imprison her. If she can, then the connections between her mother and herself, between the speaker and her own daughter, might become a form of healing, a way of loving the "life we live."

These poems and memoir are all of a piece. They trace Joan Sidney's journey to "live fully with happiness, love, and suffering." As she comes to understand, she must live with MS and the past until they are "as much a part of me as my breasts and belly—not an enemy to hate, fight against, and try to destroy." This is, indeed, the wisdom of the body that grows in spirit even as it diminishes.

— Robert Cording, Ph.D.
Barrett Chair of Creative Writing
and Professor of English
College of the Holy Cross
Worcester, Massachusetts

ONE: PRESERVES

PRESERVES

Katahdin: covered with blueberries, wild blueberries,
bushes low and thick, sprawling across the trail,
as we climbed higher. Stepping lightly from rock

to rock, across surfaces patched green with lichen, we
outstripped Dad, left him sitting on the ledge, his hand
filtering sun so his eyes could reach the top.

That was the first time he complained his chest felt tight,
years before his steps grew slower, his breath
more strained, before his heart gave in.

Superstition says, *Tragedy comes in threes.*
This is number two: always in memory you
are hiking the Carpathians, nibbling from wild vines.

You stop long enough for the camera to catch
you and your friends. I can't remember their names, though you've
told me many times. The one who married and had children,

the one who studied medicine or mathematics. I recognize
only the survivors—you and Dad.
Today, after all your losses, how can I tell you

why I drag my feet to walk? Each week the muscles tighten.
I stretch and swim and lift my legs with weights, fighting
to keep them supple enough to move me through my house.

But with every step on these wobbling legs, I know
I disappoint you. I remember how carefully you brushed

and combed my curls, tying the satin ribbon in a perfect bow.

How you stood ironing, your tears on my dress
hissing like steam, as you spoke of the world you fled.
How can I tell you: *Multiple Sclerosis?*

Blueberry day. I drive us to the Agriculture School
a half-mile from my house. Pint baskets line
the salesroom shelves, as we line up to buy.

At this moment, I know you are still grieving.
In my kitchen, you watch me sit on the stepladder
stirring six pints of blueberries with sugar,

bubbling in a stainless pot. *In Zurawno, you tell me,*
poor people came to our village with their broken-down
wagon of blueberries. They cried: "Afinys! Afinys!"

We ran with our iron pots and bought so many blueberries,
like this ... You spread your arms as wide as they'll go,
forgetting your arthritis. For days we made pies, pirogen,

jam. Our hands were black from berries, our lips and teeth
from tasting. Your grandmother, Gisella, complained: "Enough!"
She was worn out, her legs streaked from standing

over the stove. But each time the wagon came through town,
I ran out again to buy. The season was so short, the winter
so long. It was worth sacrificing a few swims in the Dniester

to be able to open the trapdoor, to climb down the wooden
ladder, and to bring up a jar of dark jam
shimmering in the kitchen light, like a field of summer stars.

POKER

At eleven years old my daughter reads me
the rules, insists we play poker
on the Oriental rug, closing both doors
for privacy. In the first deal two aces

crowd my king. I bid five, she passes,
throws out two tens. I win. Not like the first time.
Next-door in Flatbush, two sisters taught me
strip poker. With each deal they giggled, waiting

for me to show them more. We sat in a circle.
Tossed clothes in the center. A pile of shoes,
socks, hankies, barrettes began to take
the shape of girls. First to unbuckle

my belt, I slid off my woolen skirt, stretched
the turtleneck over my ears. The room
was cold. Like tonight, winter, my hair
has turned the color of coal dust and frost

laced across their windows above the cellar door.
My daughter huddles deep into her cards, her lips
parting to blow wisps of black out of her eyes.
I see myself in that other room, the radiator

coughing steam. No window quilts, no thermal panes.
I shiver, hug my shoulders with crossed hands,
down to my cotton panties, my first bra.
In their skirts and sweaters they stare. Their eyes

make me hot and cold at the same time. My cards
can't win: no flush, no triplets. They watch
my fingers unhook the bra. They stare at my secret
tiny breasts, nipples like sentries in the cold.

I hate their eyes, their laugh, their warm clothes.
Two against one and I can't stop. Nor can I win.
Not with the cards they deal me, not in
their room. I am naked in my panties

when their mother opens the door. She tells me
to get dressed, to go home, a memory that still
makes me cross my arms and hug my shoulders.
I hear the furnace hum below us in the basement,

my husband and sons gallop the stairs
outside my door. For these few moments
we sit warm and safe inside our house.
My daughter deals me another hand.

FOR THE NEW YEAR

Our rabbi tells us not to live in the past
but on Yom Kippur to remember.
How can I remember
the grandmother I never knew?

For the New Year,
Mother teaches my children to braid challah.
Side by side we weave the loaves,
watch through the oven door
how they fuse like trees at night.

We thumb black-and-white
photos from Poland. Grandmother
stands beside ten children.
Behind them her flower garden,
stripped: chrysanthemums and asters clipped
by townspeople to honor their prince's birth.

Grandma, you lean against the fence
rereading letters your children sent
from Argentina, America, Israel,
begging you to flee. You watch the old
familiar road turn black with soldiers.

BODY OF DIMINISHING MOTION

Even the saguaros,
split by lightning
or disease, die in thick armor.
Even the cactus
can't count on its red blooms.

For thirty years I denied
the day might come
when to walk across a room
would be too far.

Now shriveled,
my leg muscles will not
bear my body.

A climber's legs
once, they stretched
across rock faults, hiked
the hard way up a dike.

I slid the rope
through my fingers,
rappelled my body
rock to rock.

Back and forth
I crawl across this room,
synchronizing
opposite leg and arm.
I try to train my nerve cells

8

to reconnect, as if
there's method to disease.

The voice inside
guides: *Test of faith.*
Don't hope, expect.
Hope leaves room
for doubt.

Articles, stories, books—
every day I read how
people heal themselves.

In every cell memory.
Every pain, every emotion
imprinted and passed on.

Grandparents I never knew,
their bodies tossed
into a pit for Zurawno's Jews.

Last night in bed
my bowels erupted, spewing
across my sheets and thighs.
Was I my great-aunt in Auschwitz
dysentery draining her skeletal body?

So many voices
through me trying to speak.
Shechinah, female face of God,
free my body from their shadows.
Let me tell their stories and mine.

VESPERS

No one in church. The candles
know how to pray: they abandon themselves
in the silence until nothing's left
but the light they've become.

FAMILY HISTORY

On the first day of winter break
you argue with your kids
over ten-speed bikes, computer games,
their endless list of essentials.
To survive the week, you decide

to fill their heads with family history.
How their grandparents fled Hitler, one
or two steps ahead. How they rode
mules across the Tigris, rested halfway
on a rock, watching a peasant

test the river, beckon them to come.
They passed through cities
from Belgrade to Salonica to Cape Town,
searching for someplace welcome to Jews.
In New York City, they moved in

with your aunt. You fell asleep
in her single bed each night, woke up
wrapped in blankets on the floor.
On Nostrand Avenue, Gentiles and Jews
flourished side by side like Mr. Policano's

flowers beside the vacant lot.
You and his son Louie rode the trolley
to church some Sundays. Communion
became your word, *mazal tov* his.
For fourth grade, your parents chose

five rooms on the other side of Flatbush.
Two-family brick houses, clipped hedges.
No telephone poles to link garage roofs
like ladders to the moon, no fire
escapes for catching shooting stars,

only the hand-me-down bike
from your cousin in Forest Hills,
balloon tires and rusting spokes,
to take you back to that vacant lot
for the taste of honeysuckle.

MALKA AT NINETY

In Yiddish, your name means queen.
"Too hard to go to the beauty parlor,"
you have let your crown go
from gold to silver for the first time
since 1945, when after twenty-five months
you emerged from hiding.

Until you and Uncle Munio emigrated
and moved in across the street,
my parents refused to speak Polish.
"You're Jews, not Poles,"
the government told them.
I hated those rough, guttural
sounds I couldn't understand.
I wanted, like you, to belong
to both worlds: Flatbush,
where Coney Island and the Brooklyn Dodgers
were a nickel's subway ride away;
and the *shtetl*, where Zisl played his violin
in the street below your steps.

How did you survive
those twenty-five months, in a cellar
below the cellar of a house? Thirty-five
Jews in a space designed for twelve.
How did you breathe without a single inhalation
of fresh air? Endure without a second of sunlight?
What did you eat when the rats
stole your stockpiled flour, barley, kasha?

Late Sunday afternoons on East 2nd Street,
you'd bribe me with your fox-head stoles
to behave, letting me find them in your bedroom drawer.
We'd pretend your evergreen bedspread was the forest
where they stalked. After dinner, you'd pile
my plate with *rugelach*, and thumb-print
cookies filled with strawberry jam, powdered
sugar sprinkled on top.

Today I sit in your living room of twenty-five years,
on the twelfth floor, Miami Beach.
How many years since you touched
your oven? These days I bake
your honey cake, laced with whiskey
and walnuts. Laila, your Jamaican caretaker,
brews tea. Her name means night.
She blares *Days of Our Lives*
as we try to talk.
"*Starość nie radość*," at the elevator door
you whisper. "Old age is no pleasure."

OYSGEVEPT

The doctor told me it wasn't fair,
for my sake, to make my husband
live, that he was *oysgevept*, used up,

his kidneys worthless as shriveled peas.
Three times a week we took the bus
for dialysis, standing in the heat,

in the street, afraid
the driver would pass us by.
He cried and held my hand

when he told me
he wanted to die. *Not yet*, I begged.
No matter what, it's better here

than in the dirt. Was I too selfish?
Sixty-one years we loved each other.
I can still see the peak of his hat,

his gray wool coat, his face lighting up
when, every evening after work,
I came down the drugstore steps.

Today I think of Tante Yente
afraid to sleep with an empty space
where her husband used to be.

I don't believe in another life,
that we'll have the luck
to live again together.

Oysgevept?
God, the doctor thought he was,
not human like you and me.

BELGIUM, 1942

Your mother disappears.
Another pair of hands
pulls off your shoes and socks.
Another voice
coaxes you to eat.

You don't ask why.
Remember
your name is Micheline,
not Ida.

The family teaches you
to say grace before meals, to bow
your head and pray.

At school, the children
sing their songs.
Faraway
you see the yellow star
your mother stitched to your sleeve.

VISIT WITH THE DEAD

In the dark of early morning, my brother
Ralph trudges through first snow falling on city streets,
enters the rented walk-up, improvised sanctuary, joins his *minyan*,
a circle of ten men and women. Every day

before work, in *tallis* and *tefillin*, he bows,
rocks, chants *Shacharis*, the morning prayer,
Kaddish, to help the deceased's soul reach God, the rabbis teach.
Your body one month buried, Father, where are you now?

Believer in good deeds not rituals
you crisscrossed Brooklyn in your Studebaker
any time relatives needed a ride. You opened
your three rooms in Flatbush to welcome Mom's niece

from Argentina, who years later, married on Park Avenue
without sending you an invitation. But you
needed nothing in return. It's I who imagine
your spirit walking the waterfront

searching for your partners who cooked the books.
While they drive their black Cadillacs out to Spring Valley
where their bejeweled wives wait at bay windows,
Mom cries at the kitchen table,

knowing once again you'll come home
without a job. Ralph hides in his room,
hands covering his ears, tries not to hear
her screams, your plea: *Frances, forgive*

me. *I'll still find a job, I'm not too old.*
The haberdashery you bought in Harlem.
Mom hems slacks, for the first time, a seamstress.
Ralph waves his college books

in your face, too busy to wait
on customers or watch the register.
Because always with love,
not resignation, you forgave, you need no one

to intercede. But for the New Year, let me light
a *yizkor* candle, as if I need Yom Kippur
to make me remember your heart attack
that gave Ralph reason to return. His fingers

kneaded your back, relieved your skin-
creeping itch and let you sleep. I could only
stand outside the curtain around your bed,
not watch your body shrink to bone.

You never taught me how to let you die.
Your voice whispered insistently, until
my body rebelled, my illness setting limits.
How could I tell you now? My secrecy

a curse I couldn't call back.
I need that candle I can't find.
It's not enough to burn a bulb all night,
or let Mom light an extra in my name.

Let me sit in your bed downstairs,
in the house you helped me buy.

Let me see you in the dream I had last night:
your cheeks pink, the hollows of your eyes

fleshed out. In an almost
familiar room, you sat down beside me,
so close I could feel the heat of your hand,
smell your breath—baked apple, cinnamon.

NEXT DOOR

Oaks drag alongside the road,
weighted by yesterday's snow.
There's Frauka walking alone,
the hood of her parka
snow-lit against the trees.

I pull over. *How is he?* But before
I can answer, I see them last
summer: Frauka, and Father
leaning on Mother, wanting to believe
her will can make him well.

Sitting on the lawn,
pretending to read, I am unable
to tell them, *My legs won't walk.*
Go on without me.

Eleven years I've protected them—
Holocaust survivors—by not naming
my disease. Wishing them dead
before they'd see me in a wheelchair.

Frauka whispers, *My younger brother*
died one day before your father.
Tears rim her eyes, her slim
body shivers in the wind.
For a moment we are closer
in our sorrow than we've ever been.

TWO: BETRAYAL

STAMPS

Each stamp another country—
exotic flowers, ancient ruins,
the Etruscan vase she found
near the church in Gubbio, high above
the market flooded purple with fuchsias.

A poster from Siena reminds her
of the Palio—jeweled horses jerking backwards
at the starting line, ignoring their frantic jockeys;
the handsome Italian in skintight pants
urging her to bet on the race.

Today, Chris and I trade stamps.
She watches me display
my duplicates on her dining room table.
Afternoon light will allow her to see the stamps,
if her scooter is turned to the right angle.

Her eyes follow my hands opening her album
to the correct page, pulling back the transparent cover,
smoothing the stamps in place. Pages stretch between us
like the patchwork quilt across her legs.
I'm afraid of why I've come.

On the table, her essay, *Multiple Sclerosis
and How to Cope*. She asks how I feel,
insists I look wonderful. My legs know
the walk around our block as a sequence of stops—
how I sit on any available lawn, pretending

I'm waiting for a friend. Chris's body slumps lower
in her motorized chair, hands too numb
to make it go. Her hair is slightly grayer
than mine. Her nurse hoists under each arm,
twists Chris's torso side-to-side, fluffs her pillow.

We talk of urgency, her voice a halting whisper.
Of training caretakers to rush the daily shower,
not to let the movement from scooter
to transfer bench to shower seat,
or the scrubbing become the morning

instead of a Bach concerto or the Bible.
Letters, books, stamps.
Birds of Paradise blaze
in the black Etruscan vase
where Minerva, engraved in gold, rises.

ONE SUMMER IN CONNECTICUT

Stanley Rabinowitz snapped a photo
for a souvenir so we'd rent again next summer,
filling his farmhouse with distant relatives

from the DP camp. The photo's in an album
someplace, now missing, not lost forever
like those cross-stitched hankies Mom embroidered

when she was young in Poland, or the sepia
tints of relatives I'll never know. Our lives
as they were once, packed neatly in cardboard

boxes we stacked at the back of some closet,
until no one remembers where. But that photo—
me skipping across a field, holding hands

with Dad, strands of hair blowing across my face,
as I sucked on them. Dad listened to the sound
and seemed to disappear. It reminded him,

he said after a while, of his little
brother in Zurawno who sucked on his sleeve.
He began to whistle a lullaby, *Rozynkies*

mit Mandlen. Sucking air in to make
my whistle sound come out, I helped Dad.
If I had the photo, I would show you

how the field looked, the hay just cut
and baled, though the strong sweet smell
would be more than I could manage. The old

tractor at the edge, anchoring everything,
the border of pine trees past the field,
like a picture frame. It was so hot,

I wished I were wading in the Willimantic,
too far to reach by foot. But for then,
Dad and I entered the forest. The pine

trees protected us. For a few moments
we felt cool in that grove
which smelled so green. Sunlight

filtered through pine needles. Dad squatted down,
swept his freckled hands across thick layers
of soft brown pine, making a bed for us.

We lay down with our shoes on.
His fingers brushed the strands from my eyes
and mouth. He told me another

story of his childhood in Zurawno.
I snuggled my head across his tee-shirt,
enjoying the tickle of his chest hairs

on my neck, the steady thumping of his heart.
I fell asleep dreaming of his seven
brothers and sisters who would never

come to Connecticut or anyplace else. Wishing
they were beside us, resting under these sticky pines.
Wishing I could whistle with all my might.

NUDE

She stands under the umbrella of spray, her face
tipped up, all radiance and pleasure, eyes

closed, hands folded. She bends
her torso, early twenties I suppose, reaches

for soap on the cracked green tiles,
then begins to lather. Her hands

glide across her body, as if
outlining a well-traveled map. From under

my nozzle I soap myself and watch, wondering
how far this show will go. Steam rises

from every jet. All these women rushing
from shower to lunch to work. Am I

the only one with curiosity
to stay and look, with time to notice?

In no time, it's just the two of us: this woman
busy with her body and me, the voyeur. Her fingers

stroke her neck, stroke and lather, loving every stretch
of skin, moving down into the crease between her breasts

as if to music, her hands the instruments
harmoniously stroking each aureola, gently, patiently

plucking each nipple erect. Her eyes stay shut,
centered somewhere between billions of nerve

endings. Slipping lower, her hands circle,
stroke the thick black delta until her finger

slips inside, playing, staying long enough
to make her knees twitch back and forth,

her breath become sweet gasps. Long enough
to let me rejoice in her desire, her talent

to transport herself so deep into her body,
beyond these peeling drab-green walls.

JIN SHIN DO

Closing my eyes, I breathe in and out,
sinking deeper into my body until the room
becomes the hum of Dottie's fingers

along my legs, my chest and shoulders, forehead,
the back of my neck. Until my body rises up
to meet her healing, April sunlight on the handful

of purple crocuses beside my kitchen window.
Slowly she moves up and down, pressing out the knots.
At my feet, her fingers stall—resistance

in the toes. Over and over, she presses,
watching them spring back, as if someone else's.
I kick like a rifle, sex and anger knotted together,

my body the storehouse of every
dismissed conversation, my husband too busy
at his desk to come to bed.

Waiting, I am always waiting
for the moment we will move beyond our bodies—
when our everyday words crisscross like aspen trees

and he sees me for the first time
threading through hillsides of columbine, my body
rising high above the trees like a red-shouldered hawk.

FLAMENCO NIGHT AT CENTRE CAP PÈREFITE

Lights like fireworks explode
anemone   aurora   coral.
The orderly beats life
into his guitar. He sings
to the woman who shrieks
when someone comes near.
She closes her eyes and smiles.

Maria rolls her chair
to the middle of the crowd,
swings back & forth,
then pops up on her wheels
to show her stuff.

And now Josette, blonde
hair cropped close, glitzy
earrings, beads and pin.
At her seat, like castanets
she claps her crutches.

Alone as always, the teenage
boy hides in the dark. Eyes
half-open, lost without therapies,
not a sound from his mouth.

In the middle of this night
I am swept onto the floor.
Hands on the edges

of my footrests swirl me—
I am not dizzy from the turns.

My sea-green skirt
flares away my pain,
my shawl unfurls,
I throw open my arms
and spin, in my blood now
the music in the strings
of Juan's guitar, on the tip
of my tongue the song.

COMING HOME

The trail braids root with stone
with me dragging feet that waver
trip each other leaving the crisscross
of hiking boots waffling in the dust.

At my side icemelt sculpts sedimentary rock
rewriting history as it carves.
I snap the scene indelible. Pass
into the clearing where columbine
pose like women of the night
exposing themselves to all comers

purple yellow white
petals erect. My breast
heaves in their scent. Yellow warblers
trill beside me in the aspen grove.

Find me here in the valley
like bear claws scratched in aspen bark
or dinosaur fossils etched in sandstone peaks
or avalanche-flattened trees in rubble
where nothing grows.

BETRAYAL

I.

Charles is at my head, Ron, my feet,
Susan, my right arm. With a nickel's worth
of pressure, they support my body in its travel.

Suddenly, I'm crying on the table.
Why does it feel
as if Susan is wrenching
my right arm from its socket?

Dad tries to say good-bye—
it's Sunday. The park.
I'm holding tight as he pulls away.
I know he won't come back.

Who did Mom say she met? Who
was that man my mother might have loved
but didn't because *I was married
and it wasn't right*?
What really happened?
She was so beautiful,
her eyes and breasts
burned up the men she met.

Too late to ask Dad
about his life with women.
How many times I imagined
him and the lawyer

Mom caught him with in Yugoslavia,
hand-in-hand along the Sava,
walking past her and Tante Elsa.

In myself I glimpse his impulse
to wake before dawn, pack the rucksack,
and hike for weeks or months.
Always people to discover.
Is that infidelity?
Instead of sexual encounters, fantasies
of *what if*? Don't I always choose
men as committed
to their families as I to mine?

II.

Ron abandons my feet
to cradle my right leg that begins to travel
off the table. I am back teaching
high school, alternating days with students,
evenings and nights with Stu.
Six weeks married, forever making love.
You have too many friends,
he warns, as if I had time anymore.
You're too close to your mother.

Fire drill: on the stairs at school
my right knee buckles. Numbness
and tingling in my toes.
Three days later, I can't walk.

BETRAYAL

My body's civil war.
An auto-immune response, my cells
destroy each other, or a virus
attacking my nerve sheaths, or that New Age
theory: *dis-ease* in my lifestyle, a message
I refuse to hear that scars my spinal cord,
interrupts communication. So why
after twenty-six years do I still blame him?

Did I invent his affair
at that conference out-of-town? His colleague's
arrival before their time to go.

Or is it my anger
for all those years he disappeared
upstairs after dinner, left me
alone at the table to swallow my conversation,
as if it were dessert he shouldn't eat?

III.

On the table, off the table.
My legs are twisted in the air, my head and torso
supported by Charles and Ron. Susan, where is she?
From another place I hear my own voice shriek.
No cure for this disease, I have come
to this clinic to learn to move beyond.

Each day is more
than the few steps I can walk
or the wheelchair I resist.

I am running. A mother again,
swinging my children at the playground.
I never suspected
what was backing up inside,
hidden deep in connective tissue.
How to halt this destruction?

Again and again
I am on one table or another,
these strangers become intimate partners.
Last night I fell asleep writing to a therapist.
Why did he make my attempt to heal
an excuse to overstep? Why
did I let him touch me?

IV.

How much longer must I lie on the clinic table
before I scream? *Enough!*
I am dying in this marriage
where we sit across the table but don't touch.
Is this the message I keep cutting off?
Much more than copulation, to make love.
To caress each finger
until the hand awakens and strokes back.

If you set something in motion, it
will come back, Susan says, *like love*
from another source. But I'm tired
of everyone's advice. I show Charles
my wedding ring, Hebrew letters intertwined.

BETRAYAL

Nafshie kishura binafshaych:
My soul is tied to yours.

Ron looks too. Just back from Nashville,
he visited a childhood hill.
When his arm and leg were useless,
he drove there every day.
Dragged his body up and down, on hands
and knees, until he kicked MS.

I have no childhood hill.
There are only these tables,
these strangely intimate hands,
my husband sitting in the waiting room,
my mother living in her memories.
My body lying here, stubbornly trying
to set love in motion.

NAMING

A fat chickadee outside my window
flits from tree to tree. Her buddies

spitting sunflower shells into the snow
make me think of your last visit, Chris,

eleven years back, how you sat
in my dining room chair, intrigued

by the birds on the makeshift feeder—a sheet
of tin bolted to a rusting pole.

With a *Field Guide to Birds*,
I became your teacher. You'd drive over,

park in my garage, then drag
your body up the four steps

and drop into this chair. *Multiple
Sclerosis.* In those days, your hands

turned the pages. You held your teacup,
your fork. This morning, I chose the one you liked,

the one I bought in Delft, its handle white
with a blue windmill. These days, learning to name

BETRAYAL

this fatigue, this off-balance hesitation,
I am your student. Like you, I

need to know every name: lesion,
exacerbation, remission, remyelinate.

THE SUNDAY NEWS

Seven-fifty-five Sunday morning:
Mother on the phone.
I didn't want to miss you,
launching nonstop into yesterday's news
which has nothing to do with televised disasters.
Only from her lips can I hear
survival stories.

Boshka took me to Central Park
to meet her friends, all Jews
except for one real Pole.
On the bench we sat, remembering
our hometown, naming the streets,
the shopkeepers, the teachers
we left without "Good-bye."

Yetta finally called.
I worried she wasn't home.
Maybe they were wrong, those doctors
who know everything. Maybe
her liver cancer disappeared.

Yanka's in the hospital again.
Her brother came by her apartment,
and saw her legs and stomach so swollen,
he thought she'd die in bed.
All those years he ignored her,
now he visits every day.

Ralph went yesterday
to Long Island to give a speech,
then to New Jersey to visit "a friend."
Who, he didn't say.
I know better than to ask.

Manya drove to Peekskill with Lonik.
Now that she has her son, she forgets
she promised me. But I don't care.
Ralph will be back tonight, so
I'm cooking a chicken and soup.

My friends were surprised
you didn't come when I fell.
I was mailing you a letter
when the hurricane knocked me down.

I can't understand how strangers
mean more to you than blood.
If not for the War, I would never
have left my parents.

I don't hear much
from your children. They're busy
with school. It's your fault
they don't date Jews.
What Hitler couldn't do,
we do ourselves.

Go have breakfast.
When the stores open,
I'll look for shoes.

THREE: CASTOFFS

LEAVING

Why do you say you escaped,
Mother, when you are still
trapped among their bones?
How many have you dragged
into your Holocaust past?
Every day you are back in Poland.
Every day the Ukrainian peasants
shoot your parents and push them into the ground
you never found. Every day
someone scratches the earth for treasures
they buried behind the outhouse.
Babi Yar you say over and over.
Though you mean *Zurawno*, your world
so small, every town becomes Zurawno.

CASTOFFS

My closet: tangled hand-me-down
skirts on hangers, sweaters
scrunched on shelves. This one,
too small, dotted with outrageous
octagonal buttons, a sweater
my mother at eighteen wore in Poland.
Too good to give away, Mom repeats
each time I start to sort.

Uprooted for the summer to escape
Florida heat, she stops at my study
door, her fist hovering in the silence
between knocking and turning the knob.
At dinner she *kvetches: All day you sit
and sketch. Your feet will forget
how to walk.* Or, *They'll kill each other
your kids. Why won't you make them stop?*

Before I married, whenever we differed,
she assured me: *When you become a mother,
you'll agree.* But after inspecting George's room,
Mom shrugs and shakes her head.
Not like her house, where her fingers
filed my chaos into drawers.
There was nothing she wouldn't do,
and I let her. Evenings after school, she sat
me down to talk about my day, making me
repeat each conversation until the words
took on a second life and filled her up.

Today Mom's my passenger, riding
to Goodwill. Nonstop at eighty-eight,
oral history's her *shtik*: Aunt Lilly peeing
in the forest, wiping with shiny leaves.
Tante Elsa, Austrian Aristocrat,
fleeing on a mule. Grandpa, the cattle
dealer, refusing to leave
Zurawno, an avalanche
of memories she cannot give away.

FORGING LINKS

. . . European Jewish civilization—language, culture,
institutions—was wiped out utterly.
— Cynthia Ozick

In the early morning silence, reading *The Drowned*
and the Saved, a vision of Primo Levi
comes to me: his eyes, clouded behind spectacles, squint

as he trudges each cobbled street searching for traces
of Turin's Jews. In and out of my dreams I see their houses
usurped by neighbors, the *mezuzahs* on the doors

torn away, desecrated, though the shadows of the dead
still visit the doorposts like kisses children feel
on their foreheads long after they grow old. Late March

and it is snowing, though I know nothing will remain,
that these fat flakes are no more than memories
disappearing into trees, like my children who have left

their swing set to me and the squirrels. Each time
they return, I tell them another of my parents' Holocaust truths.
In the town of burnt corpses a peasant heats the ground

to dig their graves. It was as if all of our corpses
streamed to heaven in the full moon with its red ring.
A way to link us to that other world we'll never know.

ACHE

Over cocoa and Tylenol at 2 a.m., Jenny sits
listening to hot water travel the baseboard,
my daughter awake with throbbing teeth, my three
sons asleep, spouse snoring. Outside, voices muffled

by Thermopane, maybe the calls of owls
through trees, the light from our bay window
surprising them the way my tears surprise me.
New braces: wires threaded through brackets,

elastics crisscrossed. My daughter pulls
her swollen face away from my cool fingers.
I close my eyes to see Jenny stretching
her fingers to mallards at the pond,

pulling back before their beaks nipped.
In those days, I would have carried her
to my bed and nursed the pain away.
But now, at thirteen, she needs to sit beside me

at the table, far enough away
to be out of reach. And I need
to let go her pain. Like my mother,
I think: *Why are you so pale? so thin?*

But I stay silent. The room begins to spin
with voices, generations of mothers, mine:
When you married, why did you move out?
If not for Hitler, I never would have left

my parents. I look at Jen, face resting
in the pillow of her hands. Before the others stir
the day begins, I light my candle, welcoming
Shechinah's divine presence to heal what's broken.

MORNING SWIM

You pass me in the corridor—dark
glasses, long winter coat—attempting to steal
past recognition. Always you preferred

anonymity, slipping here and there
before my nearsighted eyes
could blink you back to focus.

But today's the first of spring, appropriate marker
to herald your return. Four months fighting
the disease two hospitals couldn't name

while it ate you up.
Yoga, macrobiotics,
something has to work.

One night last month, I dreamed you
dead, your body hollow, floating
face-down. In a circle, we morning

swimmers breast-stroked around you,
invoking the power of our pulls
and kicks to propel you on your way.

I wish you could've seen
the colors of our suits: fuchsia, turquoise,
saffron in full bloom. Sunlight

rising out of the pool, scintillating

the air above our heads. Today
I watch your legs descend

the steps, flesh to metal to water,
flinching at the chill,
your unexpected splash and shriek.

LAPS

In this marriage of water and air
always she is the beginner

teaching her hands and arms
to push away the water, to raise

her head, to breathe. Though
she swims her laps, butterflying

up and back, trying to kick loose
her leg muscles, the hamstrings

spasm, then left foot crosses right,
forces her to invent a one-legged

way to swim. No more can she
hoist her body out of the pool, or

climb the metal stairs. Instead
she sits in the hydraulic chair, waits

for someone to flick the switch.
Immobile in air,

gravity reclaims her.
In the locker room, there's

always a woman to pull up
her panties, stretch slacks, socks.

After years of early-bird swims
they know each other's bodies.

Wrinkling skin, diminishing limbs.
Nothing holds them back.

DÉPAYSÉE: UNCOUNTRIED

A robin darts branch to branch.
The rhododendron one story higher
than three years back. Lily of the valley

and pachysandra sprawl the brick walk.
Pebbles washed away, the driveway
a hazard of speed bumps no one designed.

House and yard,
nothing irreparable.
In France, where I went to heal

in a tiny mountain village,
my neighbors carried me
down and up nine stone stairs

to my spartan apartment.
Nothing could stop
my progression from ski poles

to walker to wheelchair.
Today, my neighbor
swings his pickaxe

outside my door, gouging
two trenches wide
enough for a wheelchair ramp.

I really want to do this.
Both my parents had MS.

Auger, post-hole digger, shovel.

Forty-two inches down.
He names the boulders
he crowbars loose,

lines them up on my front lawn.
I admire how gracefully
the ramp curves to marry

the driveway. Silence.
No sign of my neighbor.
Job done, he's gone

home. The boulders,
Snail Darter, Spotted Owl,
remind me where I am.

VENON, FRANCE

I have come back
to the mountains above Grenoble
where once I jogged along muddy trails,
Jean-Paul's finger at my back,
prodding me. Where once I walked
from house to house, tasting
Madame Bernard's *vin de noix*, Maria's *clafouti*.

I have come back
to study yoga with Françoise
and transform my body into light.
To sit in a circle of neighbors, as the sun
sinks into the crevice between two peaks.
To let them carry me
in my chair wherever
stairs block my wheels. Not to walk,
but like Lazarus to rise.

I have come back
to explore Le *chemin de guérison intérieure*
at l'Arche, in the Abbé de St. Antoine.
To hear Jeannette ask God to heal me
in a chapel sunlit through stained glass, stone
by stone released from five hundred
years of earth. Five times each day, the medieval
clang   reminds me to stop
and listen to magpies outshout
one another, to the donkey alone
in tall grass braying.

WITNESS

One story pressed against the mountain
patches of daylilies terraced in slate—
white clapboard, green shutters, alongside
a swimming pool where every day for forty years
I swam a mile beside Maggie
who died last month, almost as old
as her house, her children scattered
across the globe from the Congo
to Hong Kong, her husband
three decades of dust, but I'm here
remembering the morning sun
on her hair, the excitement of her voice
proposing our next trip: *Katahdin*
or white water?

The young realtor hammers in his sign.
My body heavy from the heat,
my legs too weak to lift,
I wheel myself out to the porch
in search of any breeze, and there's Maggie
bending again to her lilies. Catalpa
blossoms swirl across her lawn. All evening
I watch them fall, envying their grace,
knowing this splendor will repeat
each summer season
without us to bear witness.

LAST THINGS

She sat in a reclining wheelchair, staring
at her hands as if they could tell her
where she was. No more did she notice
her wedding ring, after sixty years
soaped from her finger to her son's
dresser drawer, "for safekeeping,"
as the nursing home required.
To spark a connection to the world
outside her room, the aide parked her
to the right of the nurses' station.
Volunteers stopped to stroke her hands
to evoke a smile. Her daughter visited
every day. On the fifth afternoon, as if returning
from a trip abroad, she smiled. *Joanie,
what are you doing here?* Six words,
a sentence, the human brain connecting
past to present. The way story after story
of her childhood in Zurawno or her three-month
escape from Hitler halfway around the world
used to tumble from her tongue, her mission
to educate her entourage of widows
walking circles in the condo pool,
or anyone who would listen.
The next moment she retreated
to a country without words.

LEGS

Once I draped you over a desk's edge,
inadvertently letting my freshman
composition class note the distance
between miniskirt and panty.

But now you force me
to grocery-shop out of town
so no one I know will notice
my blue and white parking pendant.

Most obvious imperfection,
blight on my daily life,
you dangle from your gel-cushioned throne,
daring me to bear weight.

Legs! How we have suffered
each other these thirty-four years.
When did we get so distant, so standoffish?
accepting with only a spasm whatever comes?

And yet you surprise me still
each morning at the pool,
churning waves with your flutter
kick of muscles hip to toe.

At times you even sidle up
in the locker room, letting me
pat you dry. Or slip into the proper
panty leg without crisscross,

while my helpers, suddenly unnecessary
clap and cheer. O, my
melancholy babies, come to me
and we will rock around the clock.

RETREAT

Outside, a snow-muffled boom.
Lights flicker, disappear.
Outside, snow swirls wilder.
A crescent moon
spins upside down.

These sudden unpredictable
drifts propel us past
the everyday complaints
of lovers who don't quite
meet expectations—her laugh
too giggly or repressed, his conversation
too superficial or self-centered,
his hand or hers too cold.

Disconnect! the gut urges.
Return
to where the Gihon
churns water into light.

What would it be like
to love the life we live?

NOTES

"The Greatest Love," after Anna Swir.

"Poker" and "Ache" are for Jennifer.

"Vespers" is for Colette Pilon.

"Family History" is for the Georges; *mazal tov* (Yiddish, Hebrew) means "good luck."

"Malka at Ninety" is for Malka Seliger; *shtetl* (Yiddish) refers to the tightly knit Jewish community way of life that existed throughout Eastern Europe before the Holocaust.

"Belgium, 1942" was written after viewing Myriam Abramovicz's award-winning documentary *Belgium 1942: As If It Were Yesterday*.

"Visit with the Dead" is for Ralph Seliger; *tallis* (Yiddish, Hebrew) refers to the traditional fringed prayer shawl; *tefillin* (Yiddish, Hebrew) refers to the phylacteries, two small square leather boxes containing slips inscribed with scriptural passages and traditionally worn on the left arm and forehead during weekly morning services; on Yom Kippur and other festivals, Jews light *yizkor* candles, which burn for twenty-four hours, to remember their dead.

"One Summer in Connecticut": *rozynkies mit mandlen* (Yiddish) means "raisins and almonds."

"Jin Shin Do": acupressure is an Oriental technique to release energy blocks using finger pressure instead of needles.

"Castoffs": *kvetches* (Yiddish) means *"complains"*; *shtik* (Yiddish) means literally, "a piece"; colloquially, "obsession."

"Forging Links": The epigraph is from Cynthia Ozick's "The Suicide Note," in *The New Republic*, March 28, 1988, vol. 198, no. 12, p. 35; *mezuzah* (*Hebrew*) refers to the small parchment scroll inscribed with Deuteronomy 6:4–9 and 11:13–21, and the divine name Shaddai, and placed in a case fixed to the door post of Jewish families as a sign and reminder of their faith. The lines in italics were spoken by a Holocaust survivor at Yale University's Fortunoff Video Archive for Holocaust Testimonies.

"Laps" is for all my helpers, especially Ruth Kort.

"*Dépaysée*: Uncountried" is for Tom Pike.

"Venon, France" is for Jeannette Legland; *vin de noix* (French) means "walnut wine," a specialty of Grenoble and Venon; *clafouti(s)* means "fruit cobbler"; l'Arche is a nonviolent ecumenical Christian community, one of several founded by Lanza del Vasto after his encounter with Gandhi; *Le chemin de guérison intérieure* (French) means "The Road of Inner Healing,"—it is a year-long workshop series designed by Simone Pacot.

"Witness" is for Maggie Atkinson.

"Legs," after Kathleen Fraser.

FOUR: HIKING REMOTE TRAILS

One sunny Saturday afternoon in early September 1965, we were hiking in Bear Mountain State Park: Stu, my husband of two weeks, and Steve, our *shadchen*, who'd fixed us up when we'd met at graduate school a year and a half earlier. On the spur of the moment, I'd planned the weekend camping trip, borrowing extra sleeping bags, knapsacks, a lantern. Loaded like pack mules, the three of us trudged for hours up and down a poorly marked trail. Ecstatic to be outdoors, hiking again for the first time in the year since I finished my master's and gotten swallowed up by high school teaching, including summer school, I felt I could go forever. What more did I need than bumpy earth beneath my feet leading me through forests of deciduous oaks and maples, and clear, crisp air to breathe?

"Shouldn't we be there by now?" Steve asked.

"I'm thirsty. I wish I hadn't forgotten the canteen," Stu said.

A friend had warned me that there was no water until you reached the covered lean-to campground, about a three-hour hike. "Maybe we should've taken that first fork or the second or the third. The map's not very clear, not better than the trail signs. How about an orange break?" We slipped off our knapsacks and sat down beside the scrub.

Stu was a magician with orange skins, peeling them off in two or three tries. On our honeymoon in a cabin by a lake in the Adirondacks, we ate oranges in bed, the scent still in my nostrils thirty-five years later.

Just then a hiker appeared out of the woods where we were headed. "How much further to the lean-to?" I asked.

"There's no lean-to on this trail. It's on the other side of the park."

"But my map says it's up ahead."

He looked at my friend's quickly drawn map, frowning. "Nope. Your map's wrong. If you want to get there before dark, this is what you have to do." He pulled out a pad and pencil, sketching a circuitous route miles long.

How could my map be wrong? But it was true that we hadn't seen one sign pointing to a campground. Obviously we weren't on the right trail.

"Thanks very much," Steve said, interrupting. "Forget it, Joan. I've had enough."

"Me, too," Stu echoed. They weren't smiling. Both faces shared that fed-up look as they lifted their packs, grunting. No sense of adventure, I thought. Had I married the wrong guy?

Outnumbered, I put the useless map in my dungaree pocket, turned around, and led them back to the car.

§

One morning a month later, the fire drill buzzer jerked me and my English class of twenty-nine seniors to our feet. As I raced down the flight of stairs to the front door of New Rochelle High School, my right knee buckled. Had I not been holding on to the banister, I would have fallen several steps.

The next morning I awoke to an electric tingling in my right toes. What's that about? I wondered, pulling my panty hose over toes that looked flesh-colored and normal. No time for distractions as I rushed to meet my 7:15 homeroom class and start the day teaching five straight fifty-minute classes. We were on double sessions that year while they built the new addition. Nor was there time after. I was moonlighting at my alma mater, City College, teaching Freshman Composition two late afternoons a week.

As Stu drove into the city from our New Rochelle apartment, I finished preparing my lesson on Kafka's "Metamorphosis." On the way back, I kicked off my navy-blue low-heeled pumps and began massaging my right foot. "Tired?" Stu asked. "Exhausted. But something weird's going on. Yesterday my knee buckled rushing down the stairs. Since this morning my toes have been tingling. Now they're starting to feel numb."

"If they're not better, stay home tomorrow and rest. Besides, I like your company." He smiled, not daring to take his hands off our standard shift to hug me. Stu was a fourth-year graduate student in mathematics at

Harvard. Finished with courses and qualifying exams, he was free to live anywhere as long as he saw his advisor regularly, which meant monthly drives to Cambridge.

All night I kept waking up to feel the numbness inching up my foot and leg. At six, I called in sick. "Come back to bed," Stu said. "I'll see what I can do."

"Whatever's going on, I don't like it." For the first time in my adult life, my body was out of control.

He began massaging each toe. Instead of feeling waves of pleasure, I felt terror. It was as if my toes were swollen, preventing me from sensing the touch of his fingers. I started to cry. "I can't feel."

Stu pulled me toward him and covered us with the cornflower comforter, a wedding present. "Try to go back to sleep. It's too early to call the doctor."

By the time we drove into Washington Heights late that afternoon, my right leg was numb. I could barely walk. Despite the Salk vaccine, had I managed to contract polio, the dread disease of my childhood summers?

Even my doctor was baffled. "Did you and your husband have a fight? This could be newly married hysteria." He probably wouldn't have made that speculation were my husband the patient.

"For tests," he sent me to University Hospital, the Neurology floor. The stocky young resident who admitted me promised: "We won't let you out until we get to the bottom off this."

Reassuring words. At twenty-three, I still believed in doctors, their uncanny ability to look at you, your color, your tongue, then figure out how to fix what's wrong.

Three and a half weeks of hospitalization and every neurological test—a catalogue of horrors including spinal tap, which left me with a relentless headache for several days, tilt-table x-rays after the injection of a contrast dye into my spine (myelogram), wires screwed into my skull (electroencephalogram), even several hours blindfolded and spun around for the neurologist's personal research, I found out afterwards—yielded nothing positive. "By default, you have neuritis, an inflammation of the nervous system. Don't ever again take birth control pills. They might have been responsible. Or maybe it's a virus. Pace yourself. Don't overwork." Knowing that I'd backpacked the White Mountains, my neurologist also warned, "Don't hike remote trails. You might not be able to walk back."

Diagnosis made, he began treating me with large doses of the steroid prednisone. From the first pill, I began to feel my toes, though I could tell from his raised eyebrows that he doubted such keen sensitivity. Convinced he'd found the cure, I felt reborn.

Prednisone calmed the inflammation, and two and a half months later, with physical therapy and rest, I returned to teaching, never imagining this nightmare would recur. From that time, however, it became difficult for me to stand for long periods, which meant—despite what I'd learned for my Master of Arts in Teaching degree about walking up and down the rows of desks to keep students on their toes—I'd occasionally sit down on my desk. One day my very embarrassed supervisor came to tell me not to sit on the desk, that in those days of miniskirts, my panties were showing.

§

Once off the Pill, not comfortable with a diaphragm, two months later I became pregnant using the rhythm method (a.k.a. Russian roulette). Stu and I were delighted by the surprise. It saved years of decision-making: should we have a baby now or should we wait? Except for my second son, who was planned, my next two children—a son and a daughter—also scheduled themselves. Contraceptive failures, they wanted to be born. Stu and I chose to welcome them.

Ten and a half years after my first neurological episode, in the midst of a Ph.D. dissertation on nonsexist education, I awoke to that same numbness and tingling. But this time it gripped the toes and ankles of both feet, extending all the way up my legs and pelvis. Impossible, I wanted to believe, not having touched a birth control pill. I sat up, switched on the lamp beside my bed, hoping the bizarre sensations would evaporate in the light like a bad dream.

"What's up?" Stu asked, cupping his hand over his eyes.

"I think I'm having another attack. Please help me to the toilet."

I leaned on his arm, staggering through the hallway. Safely on the toilet, I began to cry. "How can this be happening? Were they wrong? If it wasn't the Pill, what is it?"

"I don't know."

"I'm scared. Hold me." He bent over, drawing my head against his chest. But the steady thumping of his heart through his pajama top couldn't relieve my terror.

At 8:30 the next morning I called Vin Rogers, one of my University of Connecticut (UConn) professors, for the name of his wife's neurologist. Chris, I'd heard the secretaries say, had multiple sclerosis (MS).

Not knowing more than the name, "Could I also have MS?" I asked her doctor, after he had made me follow his fingers with my eyes and thumped me all over with his reflex hammer.

"Probably," he said, looking away. "It's your second major episode. There's no known cure. Go home and rest."

"Aren't you going to put me in the hospital, or at least give me prednisone? It worked wonders the last time." On top of all my obligations, after a life-changing Lamaze experience in France giving birth to my third son, I had become a certified Lamaze prepared childbirth instructor, teaching classes as many as three nights a week. I had learned firsthand to question my doctors, who had tumbled from their omniscient pedestals into the realm of human beings.

"No, go home and rest," he repeated. "Call me in a week if there's no improvement or you get worse."

I cried as Stu drove the forty-five minutes from Hartford back to Storrs. "What's going to happen if I can't walk?" For a moment, the classic MS Society TV fund-raising ad flashed in my head: a woman in a wheelchair looking helpless, on her face a forced smile begging you to donate.

"You'll recover. You did before."

"But without prednisone?" Wasn't that the magic pill that brought me back?

"He said you didn't need it."

"He'd better be right." My legs felt numb and tight. Fear for my future strangled my optimistic trademark.

"Let's give him a chance," Stu said. "You need to get well to raise our kids" (who ranged from two and a half to nine and a half). "After, it doesn't matter."

§

I was thirty-three, a Type-A Superwoman, when from nowhere came an incurable illness, a terrain where there were no maps. Aside from Chris and Vin, I made Stu swear to tell no one I had MS, as if hiding the truth would make it go away. For the first time in my life, I chose to keep a secret from my parents, who were living in Manhattan and drove to Storrs for that first weekend to help out, not to tell them what my neuritis really meant. "The only person they know with MS lives in their apartment house. She's in a wheelchair, completely dependent on her husband and her mother. Mom's always telling me, 'What a saint he is, the poor man. And such *tsuris* for a mother in her old age!'"

Why worry them? I wasn't going to wind up in a wheelchair. With rest, the numbness and tingling would disappear and once again I'd be off and running. Besides, they were Holocaust survivors, and wasn't it my responsibility to protect them from unnecessary sadness? They'd arrived in Hoboken in June 1941 after three months of fleeing Hitler, then learned that their parents, also Dad's brother, sisters, and their children had been killed. Hadn't they suffered enough?

As the weeks passed, however, my neurologist's hopelessness weighed me down. What was the point of spending hours a day analyzing research data at the Computer Center, when I'd never have the stamina to work a full-time job, especially if it meant commuting twenty-two miles from Storrs to and from Hartford at rush hour? I was ready to rationalize my way to abandoning my thesis. "What's the use?" I asked Mom, "the academic market's closed down," when Chris came to the rescue. "Go see my psychiatrist. You need professional help to deal with what you're going through."

I remember the ten-minute drive. I'm not crazy, I kept telling myself. I just need help sorting things out. When the clapboard you've built your house with begins to rot, if there's no one in your family who can fix it—I had always confided in Mom—you hire a professional. But please, God, let there be no one in the office who knows me.

I left Stu in the waiting room, while Dr. Little made good use of our fifty minutes. A slim woman around sixty, with her gray hair pulled back in a bun, she listened to my reasons for giving up, then outlined what I needed to do: "First: There's a blood test to determine if you really have MS. Call your neurologist and get it done as soon as possible. Second: Go to the Computer Center and start working on your thesis. Third: Spend time with Chris. After more than twenty years, she hasn't let MS interfere with her passion: kindergarten and first-grade teaching."

The blood test didn't happen. "Not worth the trouble, it's unreliable," my neurologist said. But Chris became my role model and intimate friend for the next twenty-four years, until her death three years ago at seventy-two.

§

Only once did Chris visit me, at the beginning of my recuperation in May 1976, though for her, walking was already almost impossible. With a hand-carved, multicolored Mexican cane, she maneuvered unsteadily the few yards from her car to my front door. Vin helped her up the single step. I wondered whether one day I too would need help entering my own home.

We sat in the dining room with Mom and Dad, enjoying Mom's prize-winning blueberry pie. Outside the bay window, birds were spitting sunflower seeds from our makeshift feeder, a sheet of tin bolted to a rusting pole. We admired their beauty, looking up their names for Chris, who needed to know: yellow warbler, tufted titmouse, evening grosbeak. Three years later Chris, who now ambulated on a motorized scooter, taught Jenny, my daughter, to read in her first-grade class, filling the room with her curiosity and courage.

But for the next twenty years, after a bathtub accident forced her to give up teaching, I was the one to visit Chris, early afternoon, when her energy level was highest, for about an hour. From her dining room, sliding glass doors opened onto the wooden ramp. California-style, a raised-ranch of open spaces: sunshine poured through walls of windows and skylights. In summer, a redwood deck off the living room vibrated with pots of pink and red geranium, purple fuchsia. Out front Vin created a patio area on the chip-sealed drive, so that Chris could sit with her visitor or caretaker and enjoy their perennial garden. On either side of the stone stairs leading to their in-ground swimming pool, clusters of flowers bloomed, their colors and variety like a perpetual fireworks display. By August, the zebra grass stood chest high, sentry to the purple coneflowers, pastel glads, sunburst shasta daisies, as Chris and I sat outside sipping iced tea. A caretaker held Chris's glass, directing the plastic bendable straw into her mouth. Her torso propped in place with pillows, she sat in her scooter, a yellow Amigo, which she hadn't operated for many years. Her hands lay crisscrossed in her lap, fingers curled like an arthritic's. Although barefoot in sandals, Chris's feet, elevated on a pillow on a plastic stool, were purple and puffy.

Besides raising three children and teaching, Chris had been a modern dancer and actor, an avid skier and tennis player. She and her family had spent sabbaticals in Italy and England. As her MS progressed, although she couldn't attend to her most basic needs, she interviewed, then trained and directed her round-the-clock staff of housekeepers, LPNs, and physical therapy students, and planned healthy vegetarian menus. Imprisoned in her body, she lived spiritually and intellectually, enjoying Public Radio and TV, books on tape, videos, her stamp collection, dictating letters to many friends, scheduling visitors regularly, and, in her last five years, studying Catholicism with Father Bill, the former president of Fairfield University.

"I never have enough time to do everything," she complained. "People assume that because I stay at home, I'm bored."

When I first began to visit, Chris was the only person I knew with MS. With so many parallels in our lives: dynamic women, juggling families with teaching careers; high achievers, demanding perfection of ourselves and our surroundings; years of living abroad with our children and academic husbands, I feared my illness would mimic hers. I looked at her both as a role model and as a portrait of dire possibilities. Putting myself in her place, I imagined I'd rather be dead. But years have passed. Chris, totally dependent physically on others, but spiritually a master, taught me there are many ways to live.

Sitting at her colonial dining room table one afternoon, Chris asked, "Do you feel the MS inside? There's something eating me all over but I'm fighting it. My mind is so alert, growing. I get angry when Vin doesn't say what he really means, when he dismisses me."

"Men," I commiserate, "are so used to taking charge."

§

Nineteen eighty four, eight years after my MS diagnosis, my secret was still intact. No one at the local public school district where I had worked for a year as Director of Curriculum and Instructional Services and

Title I Coordinator had any reason to suspect. Still a high-energy person, I juggled many hats. When the position was eliminated "for budgetary constraints," I switched to adjunct teaching at a local state university and began writing poetry almost every day. Writing was my way to control an external world that had disappointed me. But the more I wrote, the more I realized that I had no control over my best poems. They might begin with an overheard line or idea or image, an intention, but if I let go and trusted, they'd take me to a place of discovery.

At the same time, I wasn't ready to touch the subject of MS. Too scary! Besides, it wasn't interfering with my everyday life. Most noontimes I'd swim for half an hour at the university pool and be energized the rest of the day. In winter when there was enough snow, I'd cross-country ski up and down the forested trails of Mansfield Hollow, our local state park. On school holidays we'd drive up to Northfield, Vermont, to Plumley House, the 1920s Vermont senator's mansion, bought for bankruptcy taxes, and converted to dorms to sleep as many as forty at a time. We'd joined the Mansfield Family Recreation Association in 1982—the only way we could afford a second home—and did a little downhill skiing with the kids. But my joy was cross-country skiing Green Trails in my red knickers and pullover: "She skis a snow covered lake . . . her body rising high above the trees like a red-shouldered hawk."

Everything was fine until one afternoon in Miami. Stu, our children, aged ten to seventeen, my parents, who had retired to Delray Beach, Florida, and I were visiting my father's cousins. While walking a mile to the Balmoral Shoppes in Miami sun and humidity, my legs became weak and shaky. I was ashamed to tell my elderly relatives why I couldn't keep up. Like my parents, they, too, were Holocaust survivors. But they hadn't had my parents' good luck to leave Poland before the Nazis. Instead they'd spent twenty-five months hiding in a cellar below the cellar of a house. To them, their two sons who had become doctors and I were perfect. How could I shatter the reality they'd constructed, even if it was false?

While they window-shopped, Stu and I sat down at a juice bar. "Let's go back," I said. So we disappeared, taking a taxi to their condo, where our children had chosen to stay.

"Where were you?" Mom asked, arriving shortly after. "We looked all over."

"We want to swim," our kids demanded. "We've watched enough TV."

"We're going home. It's late and I'm tired," I said.

"But we want to swim," four voices echoed, the rare time they agreed on anything.

"You did what you wanted, now it's our turn," Ray insisted. Our second son, he has always pushed past the limit.

"Stu, tell them to behave. I don't have the energy for this."

"You had your chance to go down to the beach or the pool. Get into the bedroom," Stu screamed, while my relatives looked from one to another, not knowing what to say. "All four of you."

The door closed. In a minute they came out, their suntanned faces pale. They stared at me as if I'd shrunk into the tiniest Alice. Stu must have told them my secret. I wanted to put my arms around them and cry out, "I haven't changed. I'm still your mother. Don't look at me that way."

That night, I led Stu to the lagoon outside my parents' condo. Not wanting the water to carry my fury to the other condos, I whispered, "How could you have told the kids without me or my permission?"

"But you said, 'Make them stop arguing with us.'"

"That stopped them like a slap across the face."

"I'm sorry. I misunderstood."

We stood looking at the water, instead of each other. The occasional fish jumping and the mosquitoes buzzing filled the silence.

"I'm getting eaten alive," Stu said. "Let's go in."

§

79

For years I was angry at Stu for telling what was mine to tell, without me, in a place where we were helpless to comfort each other. A double betrayal: first my body, then my husband. I'd wanted to have some semblance of control over the illness and my life, which telling or not telling symbolized to me. I couldn't hear his side, how my covering up the truth from our children, my parents and friends put stress on him, too. Even our kids insisted we tell my parents.

"How can you hide it from Grandma and Grandpa? They stay with us all summer?" Dan, our first-born, asked, when we got back to Storrs.

"If it comes out, it comes out. If not, they don't need the aggravation."

I wasn't getting worse. It was the heat, I told myself, that had turned my legs to Jello. When I swam in Chris's pool the first summer we became close, she warned me to sit under the umbrella afterwards. "If you have MS, the sun's not your friend. It weakens you temporarily."

What was the other reason that kept me from telling my parents? I'd think of all their Holocaust losses, how strongly I needed to protect them, especially Mom, who had achieved her satisfaction vicariously through me, ever since I could remember. Those evenings after high school and college, when we'd sit down and talk about my day—the guys I'd met at lunch, my latest crush—or argue over my lifelong desire to teach.

"You're a born teacher," she'd say, remembering how "playing school" was my favorite game from kindergarten through sixth grade, "but Dr. Hyman says you're too smart, that you should study medicine or at least dentistry, like he did."

"Yuck, who'd want to spend every working day in people's smelly mouths?"

"Think it over carefully. Doctors and dentists earn lots of money. Teachers don't get the respect they did in Poland. When our teacher came into the room, we had to stand and say, 'Good morning, Professor.' Not in America. Here science is tops. I could have made a good living as a pharmacist, like I did in Zurawno. But when we escaped Hitler and moved in with my sister, who gave me work? My Uncle Aaron. For pennies he hired me to slave in his jewelry store.

"Fifteen months later, you were born. I stayed home. Such a poor eater! What I pushed in, you spat back. No one helped. If only my mother had lived to see you. I'll never forget how she cried when I left for Belgrade to marry your father. 'Mama, I'll come back. It's not far, you'll come visit me.' 'No, Fanka, I'll never see you again.' And that's the way it was."

§

Looking back over the past, I realize that Stu and my kids were right, that telling my parents would have allowed us to confront MS and grieve together, but I wasn't ready. I still unconsciously hoped that by not telling them I had MS, it would go away. With Mom, who tended to think she was always right, that she could solve any problem—and if you disagreed, she'd get insulted—I feared her taking over my life by wanting to do everything, "to make it easier."

I appreciated Mom and Dad's help, especially in the years from 1972 through 1976, when, having moved to Storrs, Connecticut, I juggled babies, young kids, doctoral studies, and teaching Lamaze prepared childbirth classes. Mom had the knack of stepping into my kitchen and filling it with the smells of freshly baked challah, kugel, strudel; she changed diapers and bathed babies, enjoying every chance to kiss and hug her grandchildren, while Dad pushed the tandem stroller with Jenny and Larry around Storrs, disappearing for hours every day. But as the children grew up, Mom became more critical and demanding. "Why do you waste your time writing? With a Ph.D., you could get a job." Or, "Come walk with us. You spend too much time sitting at your typewriter. You'll forget how to walk."

How can a body forget how to walk? Isn't it like swimming or riding a bicycle once mastered, yours forever? One hot summer afternoon in 1985, I started down my hemlock and oak treed street with Mom and

Dad, turned into the dead-end circle, walking ten minutes total before my legs began feeling unsteady.

"I'd better get back to my poem," I said, knowing I'd never make it the mile around our neighborhood, still ashamed to let them know the truth.

"The walk will be good for you," Mom said. "Your writing will wait."

"No it won't," I said, turning toward my house while they continued straight. "You walk for me."

How I envied them, in their late seventies, every day walking miles, still holding hands like newlyweds, after fifty years.

§

Because of my secrecy, after my father's heart attack and triple by-pass in November 1985, each visit to Delray Beach left me tense and worn, especially when Dad was in the hospital for a new crisis, his heart unable to pump fluid out of his lungs, or the dialysis three times a week. After walking the labyrinthine hospital corridors, and after arguing with Mom over why I couldn't give up my Storrs life and move in with them, I'd return home with my legs as rigid as a robot's.

Ralph, my brother, urged me to tell our parents, not to let them continue thinking, "She doesn't care enough. She could stay longer." But how could I tell them now? I'd waited too long.

Those almost monthly visits stretched across two years, and each time I expected this one to be our last together. Toward the end, Dad lay in bed under his quilted comforter, shivering in flannel pajamas. "Come sit," he whispered. "Who knows how much longer I'll be here?"

I sat on the bed holding his icy hands. Once his hands could open any jar no matter how tight the lid, could break an apple in half; now weak and shriveled, like the rest of his body, a shell of pain.

"I don't want your children to remember me like this," he began to cry. I reassured him as I cried too. Even then I knew I was crying as much for me as for him. There was too much loss. My beloved father, just turned eighty, was dying of heart failure, of kidney failure, his body broken beyond repair. His helplessness mirrored my worst nightmares: that one day soon I might become totally dependent. Would my children regard me as a helpless, pathetic victim, instead of their spunky, adventurous mom?

§

Dad died in December 1987. With my two youngest, Larry and Jenny, I flew south to visit Mom during the February school vacation. After leaving home at two in the afternoon, a series of flight delays and plane repairs brought us into Ft. Lauderdale at 12:30 in the morning. Exhausted, I still had the car rental pick-up and an hour's drive to Mom's.

We passed an empty wheelchair, and I plopped down in it. "Who wants to push?" After years of resisting even the thought of assistance, I realized that this wheelchair was there for me. Effortlessly, it brought me to the shuttle bus stop where, until the bus arrived, I sat and rested, then climbed aboard.

When we finally arrived at Mom's condo, "You look awful!" she said. "I never saw you looking so terrible!"

Immediately, I felt my legs tighten. I could barely walk those few steps to the bathroom.

The first few days I did nothing but swim outdoors, read underneath a palm tree by the lagoon, and eat out with Mom and her friends. "Thank God, you look a little better. There's too much pressure from your writing. I worry for your legs."

"My writing helps me understand what's happening to my body and to take control."

"But you're getting worse. I can see you walked better a few months ago. You have to stay and live with me."

How could I contradict the truth of Mom's observation? But I felt myself shrinking, becoming a helpless little girl. "Please stop, you're swallowing me up."

"You'll see, your children will always be your children."

§

After twelve years of covering up the truth of my illness, I had to tell her. I was tired of Mom's constant criticism, her fears, and her Holocaust-related view that the world was a dangerous place, which magnified my stress and my fears for the future. But she was sitting in the tweed recliner, Dad's chair. I pictured him returning from dialysis, drained of bodily poisons and energy as well, barely able to lower himself into the chair, his breathing heavy, his color gray. Go easy, I warned myself, she's had it very hard: his illness, now living alone for the first time in her life.

I began to tell Mom what my neuritis meant. "When you recently said, 'You have bad nerves,' you were right. The fatty tissue insulating my nerve sheaths is scarred. My nervous system is like a roomful of electric wires stripped thin, likely to short-circuit instead of conducting. I never know if I'll be able to walk several blocks without resting. That's why I stopped walking with you and Dad. I didn't want you to see I was having trouble."

"I thought you didn't love me anymore. I'd cry, and Dad would say, 'Don't cry, you still have me.'"

"He really loved you, Mom. And so do I." I reached for tissues, shocked that my trying to protect them had caused such pain. "Let's sit by the lagoon."

It was sunset, the time when birds glide or flap past nonstop, as thousands of ibis and egrets transformed the tiny island into snow-covered shrubs. Near us, a blue heron dipped down into the water. A duck and her five ducklings swam to shore, then quacked their way up to our chairs.

"I should have brought old bread, like I do most nights," Mom said. "See how smart they are, ordinary ducks."

§

"Why do you allow your legs to tighten when your mother worries about them?" Dottie, my therapist, asked when I came back to Connecticut. "No one but your mother believes you're so limited physically."

Slowly I am recognizing all the choices I've made and the power I still have to choose. Raised in a community of Holocaust survivors, I spent most weekends either visiting or being visited by my father's cousins or my mother's sisters and their families. As an adult, knowing the sorrows they suffered—only this lucky handful escaped—I believed I had to be perfect, to bring only *naches* to my parents and relatives, and, in this way, compensate for their losses.

In *Children of the Holocaust*, Helen Epstein interviewed second-generation Holocaust survivors in order to better understand herself. One woman echoed my obsession: "I felt chosen to strive for a full life and make up for my parents' losses. I felt an obligation to my family who perished and to my parents who survived . . . . I felt that my life wasn't entirely my own . . . . I didn't want to let any of them down. I wanted them to be proud of me."

§

I sit facing Dottie. Her questions lead me back to Joanie, the good girl, four and a half years old, before she started school. She has light brown curls, a clump of curls tied in a pink bow at her crown. She is wearing a Scotch-plaid skirt, a starched and ironed white blouse. Her shoes are black patent leather, her socks white, scalloped at the ankles.

The good girl does whatever her mother says. Mother's voice squeezes Joanie's ankles like black fists. It forces her to sit still. How can Joanie fight Mother's voice? It's always telling her what to do, always insisting it's right: "Don't go by yourself to France. You'll give Stuart an excuse to find another woman. Don't write poems, they're a waste of time. Writing is a black hole, my dentist said."

Mother's voice becomes a knotted golden thread inside Joanie's gut.

It never breaks. Biblic, it connects to the Jewish tradition of mothers growing old beside their daughters, living in their house. Mother is very afraid that if Joanie goes away, she won't come back.

The golden thread travels through Joanie's body, tightening around her neck, her fingers, her stomach, all the way down to her toes: a tiny golden rope around each toe, tied in a tiny knot.

"What can Joanie do to get rid of the golden thread?" my therapist asks, bringing me back.

"She can get very angry, so angry that her anger creates new poems to unknot that golden thread."

I feel energy like electric current coursing through my body, nerve cells covered with insulation, their myelin sheaths regenerated and intact. I see myself walking quickly, in the old way, one foot in front of the other.

§

In *Illness as Metaphor*, first published in 1978, Susan Sontag argued that today's "psychological theories of illness are a powerful means of placing the blame on the ill." Debunking the myths that people cause their cancers, e.g., by holding on to deep resentments or by inadequate self-love, or that cancer comes as a curse or punishment, Sontag urged people to seek appropriate medical treatment as soon as possible after diagnosis; that for many, cancer was a highly curable disease.

Dottie and I talked about the difference between "blaming the victim" and learning to nurture one's self. "You can't negate the fact that MS is a virus, that it is physiological." But, since neurologists still offered no treatment in the late eighties, no maps, she kept coming back to "self-love and self-acceptance. Don't hate your legs for disappointing you."

How do you move beyond the pain of progressive loss, which demands an on-going grieving, a fluid coming-to-terms? Like writing, multiple sclerosis unpredictably takes its own turns and makes its own timetable. But MS is sneaky. Just when I think I've figured out a way to stop its course by creating my own map—over the years a witches' brew of psychotherapy, acupressure, acupuncture, physiotherapy, massage, swimming, meditation, visualization, diet, and confrontational writing—I catch myself in the mirror, swollen half-moons under my eyes, complexion pale; I limp more; I force myself to scrutinize my calendar and scratch out any commitment not absolutely necessary; I reorder my priorities and sit myself down in front of my computer, as my world narrows, to reach out and write.

I think of what the photographer Dorothea Lange said about the impact of polio at age seven on the rest of her life. It left her with a withered leg and a limp. "I was physically disabled, and no one who hasn't lived the life of a semi-cripple knows how much that means. I think it perhaps was the most important thing that happened to me, and formed me, guided me, instructed me, helped me, and humiliated me. All those things at once. I've never gotten over it and am aware of the power of it all." But until beginning this essay, I would have insisted that MS wasn't guiding me, instructing me, or helping me, though I sometimes felt humiliated as I limped to my destination. Because of and in spite of MS—its vulnerability and stress, the fatigue, the diminishing mobility—I am learning to take charge of my writing and my life, reaching toward the limits of what's possible.

I am living healing, as opposed to cure. According to Deena Metzger, poet, playwright, novelist, and psychotherapist, "Cure is supposedly a one-shot deal: you cut the cancer out, you do a bypass operation, whatever it is and you think you have fixed the situation. But if the elements which caused the illness are still there, it can occur somewhere else, or in a different form. And so healing has to do with constantly attending the process by which you altered the circumstances that gave rise to the illness." After her mastectomy, she traded her frenetic Los Angeles life for the peace and natural beauty of Topanga Canyon.

In 1991, with nine others at the Omega Institute in Rhinebeck, New York, I spent five eight-hour days in Deena's "Writing for Your Life" workshop. Except for the one physically healthy person accompanying her friend with advanced cancer, we were all struggling with chronic illnesses.

By then, no longer benign or invisible, the MS had progressed. But instead of using canes for balance and support, I walked with my bamboo-style cross-country ski poles. At mealtimes, I drove up the steep hill to the dining hall, parking alongside the kitchen staff's cars, then entered through the side door.

Three times a day we came together to discover and share the stories our diseases were trying to tell. Again and again, in response to questions Deena posed, my multilayered story unraveled: a mix of the predictable Holocaust grief, plus anger at Stu for making us leave France after his sabbatical year in August 1979, an ongoing sense of loss. Venon, a tiny mountain village above Grenoble, had become my place of healing from that second exacerbation. Here the miracle happened. Little by little, I began to hike again. To jog. To cross-country ski fifteen kilometers. With visitors and friends, I wandered the mountainsides and forest trails.

Spontaneous remission? With MS you never know. But during that year in France, embraced by my new community, I felt stronger than ever before.

Suppose I'd resisted family pressures to go back to Connecticut— where an unemployed life in a university town left me financially dependent as well as professionally cut off—and insisted we stay "forever"? Would my more assertive and authentic life, one which paid attention to my innermost needs, have let me remain a cross-country skier and hiker?

§

March 1993: After weeks of rain and flooding, the sun made its timid debut, flickered, and faded out. From my window in Venon, this tiny mountain village, I watched fog swallow Grenoble below. For the moment, just being here was enough.

My husband and I have come back to France for his one-semester sabbatical. At first, to help me in and out of the car, he lifted my spastic legs, then rushed to set up my green rolling walker with its rubber grippers on each side like bike handlebars. He grocery-shopped, cleaned, and drove me to my medical appointments. In exchange, I cooked and invited our ever-widening circle of friends to elaborate American-style dinners.

At the general practitioner's, I was unable to climb onto his examining table, so the doctor played elevator, and with my hands around his neck, he lifted me up. To my dismay, after having come to France to overdose on fatty cheeses, exquisite wines, multi-course dinners with meat and fish smothered in delicate sauces, he told me that if I strictly followed the Kousmine diet—rich in polyunsaturated essential fatty acids (extra-virgin oils, cold-pressed), organic whole grains, fruit, vegetables, nuts—I'd feel better and become more independent. While he had no guarantees, he believed the illness would stabilize.

§

September 1993: Seven months later I was living in Venon on my own, owning and driving a used Peugeot, teaching English and history in an international school two afternoons a week, and using my ATM card from our joint Fleet account to make up the difference.

Convinced that I would heal my disease, I let MS give me permission to remain in France. With Larry and Jenny away at college, and Ray and Dan independent at graduate school, I was shocked when Larry and Jenny called to protest, insisting, "You don't have the right to be away from Storrs, even if we're not there anymore." Probably they were afraid that separation signified a troubled marriage. But Stu knew that after all these years of sticking by him while longing for a more exotic life, I wasn't budging. He also knew that if our marriage was to last, he had to let go.

Most distraught was, of course, Mom. "You'd better come home right away, before Stuart finds another woman." Or, "Your mother-in-law is very upset with you." There she was again, trying to strangle me with her golden thread.

"Ma, my doctor says I'm getting stronger. And Stu's behind me one hundred percent. But if you're calling to aggravate me, please don't call again."

What a relief to have said that! I didn't care what either Mom or my kids said or thought. All that mattered was Venon, and that Stu understood.

For the next eighteen months—the first time in my life—I lived entirely on my own, with occasional honeymoon-like visits from Stu. Still dependent on ski poles or my rolling walker, how did I manage?

Each drive down the mountain was an adventure, 5.2 kilometers. Like Paul Newman on a racetrack, I hugged the inside as the skinny two-lane road spun round and round. Le Perroud, Cul Froid, Pré Bousson, Venon la Ville, Le Planchon, La Serraière—hamlet after hamlet flicked by, a mix of old farms and new chalets, until I passed La Faurie, then the final *virage* and I joined cars racing to the autoroute.

"Move over to the left lane immediately," Michèle, my first Venon friend from 1978, advised. "Behind the wheel, the French go crazy. Your left exit comes up quickly and they'll never let you in."

The speed limit was 130 kilometers, over 81 miles per hour. Gières, my entry, was low traffic, so I floored the gas, passed into the left and ignored the honking cars ultimately passing me on the right, then cutting in front, each driver giving me the finger. Four minutes more and I negotiated the handful of city streets in the neighborhood of my school. The principal let me pull into the schoolyard, park in front of the cafeteria entrance where I taught a handful of sixth- and seventh-graders. I honked and immediately the young custodian came out to turn my car around. Without power steering in my automatic sedan, I appreciated the energy he saved me.

Once a week, I phoned my grocery order to the organic supermarket two towns away. On her way home from the university, a neighbor picked up my cartons, then delivered—and without my asking—shelved and refrigerated everything. Two hours every Thursday afternoon, another friend's *femme de ménage* cleaned my three-room apartment. She came not for the money, but out of compassion for my condition, since both her husband and his cousin had MS.

Long ago Chris told me how the disease brought unexpected blessings, which I began to understand. "People want to reach out to one another, but either they don't know how or need an invitation." MS became that invitation to both friends and strangers.

As promised, Colette, my landlord who lived in the main body of her alpine chalet, on the other side of my wall, washed my laundry in her basement machine, took out my trash, and came by most days for tea and talk—not everyday chatter, but to discuss questions like: "Why do you think you are here in this life?"

Back then, what would I have answered? to write? to teach? to map my way to healing, then to lead others along the trail?

With Jacqueline, another close friend, we meditated at five p.m., my knees on the rug, buttocks against the tiny hand-carved oak bench I brought back from a Zen retreat. In addition, before our weekly yoga class in the Venon community prefab, the three of us discussed what was going on with our families—not to cut them out of our lives, but to give them their independence as we reclaimed ours.

"I spent my youth fighting for causes," Colette said. "But I have come to realize that all change begins with me. As I look within and listen, I become calmer and act to resolve conflict, instead of escalating it by my old pattern: screaming, demanding my way, always needing to be in control. As I change, the world around me has to change in accommodation." Isn't this the ripple effect, ultimately the way to world peace?

One day Colette drove me to l'Arche, a pacifist, ecumenical Christian community—one of several founded by Lanza del Vasto after his encounter with Gandhi—where she had studied *Vers un chemin de la guérison intérieure*—Toward a road of inner healing. Under the centuries-old linden tree, we sat in the courtyard of this medieval abbey, talking with her friends who every year renewed their vows to their spiritual and communal lives. In exchange for living rent-free, they were restoring the historic abbey, stone by stone. To augment their income as well as to welcome strangers into their community, they offered weekend and weeklong work-shops, also ongoing retreats. Their food—all summer, vegetables from their organic garden; all year, hearty soups, whole grains and legumes, pastas, freshly baked crusty sourdough bread—nourished and satisfied. That afternoon I signed up for the yearlong inner healing series.

Only Michèle, a Jewish mother very much like Mom, wasn't happy with my independent lifestyle. She told Colette, "First I worried for Joan, but now I worry for Stuart."

§

July 1994: Since neither my four children, busy with summer jobs or graduate work, nor my mother could visit, I returned to Storrs for seven weeks. To ease the transition, Georges, my French physical therapist and masseur, will visit for three weeks. "Don't worry about missing France. I'll be with you soon." But once back, instead of continuing daily meditation and yoga, I ignored my inner life. Each day became a frenetic to-do list of errands, proving to no one in particular that I could do more than most healthy people. When Georges arrived, I began an orgy of dinner parties to introduce him, as if he were a debutante needing to make a splash. Then we took a car trip to Ottawa for a nephew's bar mitzvah, with a tour of Montreal for Georges.

"I don't like him," Mom complained. "He expects you to pay for everything. When we stop for lunch, why doesn't he treat, or at least pay for himself?"

"He's our guest, besides he gives me free massages. Would you like one, too?" On the surface, I refused to get sucked in, not even when Mom came crying: "Did you hear what he said? 'Mrs. Seliger, you have a good appetite.' What's it his business how much I eat?"

"Don't go back to France" was Mom's continuous refrain. "Who needs people like him?" This upset me. Despite my ten months of inde-pendence, on a level I hadn't yet mastered, I was Mom's little girl wanting to please her. Fortunately, in my top drawer, tucked into my passport, was my return ticket. Also, in addition to my part-time teaching at the international school, this year I would teach the first creative writing course in the English Department at l'Université de Grenoble III—jobs I couldn't get in Storrs—the ammunition I needed to make my escape from Mom possible. But why, at fifty-one, should I have to justify to my mother my right to choose? my right to lead a separate life?

§

While Mom walked behind, Georges pushed me in my Quickie, lightweight manual wheelchair that my health insurance paid for in 1992, when already I couldn't manage long distances. It was a mile and a half to Chris's. With my ski poles or rolling walker, bushwhacking the overgrown shortcut through the woods would have been impossible. The winding roadsides were shady, lush with oaks and hemlocks. No longer did I worry that a neighbor would see and judge me imperfect because of MS. With my secret years out—as my limp became as much a part of me as my eyeglasses—I had gained an unexpected freedom.

Georges wheeled me up the wooden ramp to Chris's dining room's sliding doors. How long since my last visit? A year? The past winter she had caught pneumonia, was hospitalized and almost died, Vin said. In a voice that had become a whisper, Chris haltingly related a story her dental technician had told her about "a woman from Storrs with MS who left her husband and ran away to France. 'You'd better watch out,' I warned. 'We women with MS are wild.'"

§

August 22, 1994, our twenty-ninth wedding anniversary: For the first time, Stu and I wouldn't be together celebrating. But bless him for letting go, for understanding that nothing would keep me from my next adventure.

I rushed back to France in time for the first of three five-day sessions, *Vers un chemin de la guérison intérieure.* A friend drove me to l'Arche, ninety minutes from Venon, in the turreted medieval village of St. Antoine l'Abbaye. We climbed the stone stairs, she pushed open the heavy wooden door, and we entered the long stone corridor, our footsteps reverberating in the silence. I was glad for the rubber tips hushing my ski poles. Caught by this feeling of sacred space, I stopped to admire the ceiling, stories above. After my crazy Connecticut summer, being here was a blessing, an opportunity to turn inward and get back on track.

My room was large, with a single bed and lamped night table on one wall, a bureau on the opposite wall, a sink, and a spacious table and straight-backed chair facing the courtyard and vegetable garden. Twice a day, our group of sixty met next door to listen to Simone tie Scripture to our daily lives, enhanced by her psychotherapist colleague who illuminated anecdotally her clients' healing stories. Once a day, our discussion group of ten met down the hall in the kitchen of Jeannette, our facilitator, to process. Out of eight possible facilitators, Colette advised me to choose Jeannette, one of the co-founders of this community, for her wisdom and kindness. In her early seventies, gray hair in a bun, Jeannette embraced each of us, listening without judging or manipulating, offering me a new way to love.

As the days passed, I realized I was the only Jew in this ecumenical Christian community. Jeannette and other members of l'Arche who have studied Hebrew and learned Israeli folk-dancing asked me about my roots. After years of putting aside my Judaism, the way my children did after their bar and bat mitzvahs, I had come to a medieval abbey to reclaim my heritage as I walked the road to inner healing.

In my dreams, I am always walking: no ski poles, no rolling walker; just one foot in front of another, the way we humans—*homo erectus*—cover ground. But in this abbey of labyrinthine corridors and gigantic flights of stairs, I depended on the strong arms and legs of the community in order to get up and down to meals and showers. Seeing me in the archway, men appeared, asking me to put my arms around their necks while they cradled my legs and galloped the wide staircase, either dropping me gently into my wheelchair and whisking me to a table in the garden, or standing me in front of my rolling walker on the first floor. Their attention and caring made me feel blessed.

At our session, Simone, who had developed the course, told us, "Open the door, the window to your heart. You are here because God has knocked at your door to open what's closed, blocked, chaotic." My eyes filled. When was the last time I thought about God without feeling abandoned? Often when I visited, Chris would tell me how praying made it possible for her to cope with her complete loss of independence, even to view her illness as a blessing in the sense that it has surrounded her with a twenty-four-hour entourage of loving helpers.

"Learn to be happy in your limitations, not to seek perfection but to see clearly." Why was I always killing myself to be Superwoman, Ms. A+: baking chocolate chip cookies for my kids, then racing off to the University of Connecticut for my Ph.D., then three nights a week teaching Lamaze prepared childbirth classes? Even as the mother of four, I was still that little girl needing to please my parents by pleasing everyone else. But Simone was right: MS was forcing me to face my physical imperfections and to welcome who I am, to experience the full range of human emotions. I had the right to get angry at my mother when she yanked her golden thread or to feel sad that MS was robbing me of a normal, healthy life. That in order to be loved, I didn't have to be Mom's good girl or "Little Mary Sunshine."

"Live fully: with happiness, love, suffering. Name and pass through your suffering." Over the years, I have been learning to "accept the unacceptable," to live with MS as much a part of me as my breasts and belly—not an enemy to hate, fight against, and try to destroy.

"Let go of specific expectations for healing; there is no magic cure." For how many years have I been chasing the elusive cure for a disease that science calls "incurable"? How much money do I continue to spend on alternative or experimental treatments that insurance won't cover? How much time and energy do I squander, both for me and my husband, who is my long-distance driver?

"Those times when your burdens become too heavy, offer them to God." Simone gave us some of the words, and I filled in the blanks: "God, help me to accept that today I can't walk."

"No one has the right to possess someone else, to practice emotional blackmail." Not even Mom, who telephoned frequently, repeating: "Your children tell me Stuart's lonely—he'll find another woman. Your children will forget you."

Once again, I began to protect myself from Mom's manipulation, a lesson I kept having to relearn. "Ma, please don't call unless you have good news."

"You don't have to listen to all the suffering of others, nor to use the illness for protection from that. You have the right to protect yourself without the illness," the psychotherapist said in a private meeting with Jeannette and me.

Simone cited Martin Buber, that everything begins with yourself; you end with love.

§

I returned to my Venon apartment, ready to work with Colette and Jacqueline, putting these new understandings into daily practice. Meanwhile, each day for the next two weeks, I phoned my director at the international school asking for my teaching schedule, and each day he put me off, until: "The building's being renovated, so the cafeteria's no longer available for your classes. Since there aren't any first-floor rooms, we've hired someone else."

"How could you? It's my job." But after years of adjunct teaching in American universities, I understood that without a contract, one had nothing.

I hung up the phone in my neighbor's kitchen, and as if in a trance, stared at the onions she was dicing. My eyes began to water.

"Unbelievable!" she said, having understood my end of the English conversation.

"At least I still have a course at the university." Creative Writing, my *cours à option* in the English Department, two hours a week for ten weeks this fall. In a few minutes, my income had shrunk from $8,000 to $800. Barely two months' rent.

After dinner, I drove the winding road connecting our houses, whose shortcut would be a five-minute walk through her hedge, across the street and up my steep driveway. It was dark as I transferred my ski poles to my right wrist, holding on to the stone banister with my left hand, and began to negotiate the uneven stone stairs. Giant stairs, each one requiring me to put one foot, then the other foot next to it, balancing like a baby learning to walk, before tackling the next. When I reached the fourth of nine, the light, triggered by an electric eye, kicked on. At the top I paused, anxious to talk with Colette. What will this mean, this first roadblock to my independent French life? But her wooden shutters were drawn and locked, her front door impenetrable as a medieval chateau.

Over the next days, Colette explained why her daughter, a homeopathic physician in Lyon, moved back home with her preschooler and infant daughter; why before nightfall, they barricaded themselves in the house in case the crazed partner she had fled should come after her and her daughters, but tonight I was unprepared. For the first time in my year alone, I felt uncertain. If you're walking in the right direction, shouldn't every door be unlocked? Or is having to find the key once in a while part of the adventure?

In the silence of my living room, I lit my handmade candle from l'Arche, white with a purple wildflower pressed inside, intending to meditate. But instead of counting my breaths, focusing on the "In one-two-three-four, out one-two-three-four," I prayed: "Please let me stay on this healing path."

Hearing the words reminded me why I had come back: to heal,

which, I'm learning over and over, isn't a synonym for cure. Although I'd sacrifice almost everything—short of "my immortal soul," my husband and my children—to make the scar tissue that replaced my myelin sheaths soften and return to normal nerve cell insulators, I think back to Deena Metzger's workshop and remember that "healing" means much more than "cure," which translates only to freedom from a particular disease and its symptoms. "Healing" brings harmony of body, mind, and spirit; healing reflects inner peace which radiates outward, attracting others to our light; healing allows us to live fully in the present, unburdened by our disappointments and mistakes of the past or fear of the uncertain future.

For one of my Storrs friends, whose lungs are blocked by chronic bronchitis and who can breathe in and out at 30% normal capacity, "Healing is being able to function as best I can from minute to minute."

I phoned Stu in Connecticut with my devastating news. "Don't be too disappointed. I wasn't counting on your income to pay the mortgage."

He said he had called a few hours before, but I wasn't home. "My old Grenoble research group offered me a visiting position for second semester." His voice—"Stuart's a crooner," my mother-in-law said—still soothes and charms me. Was it "Fly Me to the Moon" or "Aura Lee" that thirty-five years ago had swept me off my feet?

§

Christmas vacation, December 1994: Instead of taking a break and relaxing in Venon between semesters, awaiting Stu's arrival, I decided to go back to the States for five weeks. Mom was pressuring me to visit her in Florida. "I haven't seen you since the summer. Don't you miss me and your children?" Of course I did, especially when my friends invited me to their family gatherings. Often I sat around their tables overflowing with pâtés, roasted duck, beef filet, *saumon en croûte*, *gratin dauphinois*, *gratin de légumes*, and wines to accompany each dish. There were always specially cooked organic entrées to fit my strict Kousmine diet. How I wished my children were still young enough to be at my side! I thought back to 1978–79, our first time in Venon, when Jenny, Larry, and Ray had attended the village's two-room schoolhouse, and Dan the middle school in Gières with the next-door neighbor's son. So many of my friends' children had been their friends. The year had been one birthday party after another. Now I sat surrounded by these same children turned adult like mine, but still close enough, even from Paris, to return home for festivities. "Are you comfortable?" they asked, bringing me cushions. "What would you like to eat?" They clucked around me like mother hens, as if I were the baby chick. How could I not feel at home in Venon? And yet . . .

At the same time, because I missed my family, I tried to juggle living on two continents. That Christmas I flew to Boston, hopping to Storrs, then two weeks to visit Mom in Florida, then back to Storrs like a displaced kangaroo looking for her habitat. During part of the time we visited Mom, Jenny and her college Klezmer band were on their South Florida synagogue tour. On what felt like permanent jet lag, my body had stopped sleeping more than two or three hours a night, so why not drive through torrential rains, then hang out till 2 a.m., stamping my feet to the horas I could no longer dance to? Besides, stamping covered up the leg spasms that were also jerking me out of any sleep that sneaked up on my body.

For the first time in the thirty years I've had MS, I felt pain. But no one prepared me for this; no neurologist, no physical therapist, no alternative health-care provider, no article I read ever mentioned this excruciating pain that comes each time one of my leg spasms and cramps up to my chest, stifling my breath.

Instead of telling me to stop or at least slow down, my Florida acupuncturist gave me stinky Chinese herbal pills to swallow when the pain became "too intense." Too intense? What could be too intense for a woman who, using *l'Accouchement sans douleur* (Painless Childbirth), sailed through her last two labor deliveries with only an occasional ice chip?

I began swallowing pills every three hours, and instructed Dan, who was studying in Cambridge, to buy me a caseload in Boston's Chinatown. Having resisted drugs ever since that initial prednisone treatment series, I was convinced that herbs function differently, without potential side effects.

"But don't herbs come from the same plants as traditional drugs?" my Yale neurologist once asked.

"Bruce, if my acupuncturist claims they're harmless, she must know." I was on a first-name basis with all my health-care providers, but although I aggressively interrogated and contradicted my neurologist, I accepted as gospel anything my acupuncturist, homeopath, and craniosacral therapists said. At least they had tools to try. Except for my annual check-up at Yale since 1986, after so many years of waiting, hoping that any day neurologists would discover both the cause and cure for MS, I'd given up on traditional medicine. In 1992, before going back to France, I refused to consider daily Betaseron injections, the first just-FDA-approved treatment to cut down on MS exacerbations. "People on the Internet said it has major side-effects: depression, which has already led to four suicides, as well as severe flu symptoms. Besides, Bruce, didn't you tell me that after fifty I'm too old to have another exacerbation?"

By the time we arrived at Logan Airport, I was too weak to go to the bathroom alone. My daughter-in-law, Ray's wife, wheeled me into the handicapped stall, but called Stu to the Women's Rest Room to transfer me to the toilet seat. He lifted while she pulled down my pants and panties. I was grateful for their help; also that Stu was on a one-semester leave from UConn, teaching and researching with his former colleagues in the Math. Department at l'Université de Grenoble I.

How I survived the flight, with its three-hour layover in Brussels in the middle of the night, my mind refuses to recall, replaying only our friend picking us up at the Lyon airport, then with Stu carrying me in my wheelchair up the stone stairs, and Colette following us into the apartment. She brought me a metal bedpan, and for the next week Stu was my day and night nurse as I refused to consider Michèle's suggestion that I go to the hospital to be treated for this full-blown exacerbation, my first in nineteen years. Remembering the nightmarish battery of tests, including spinal tap, which is standard for any neurological admittance, followed by high-dosage steroids, was enough to keep me here.

"Don't you want to go back to Connecticut?" Colette asked.

"No, this is home," I answered without hesitation.

She hugged me, kissing both cheeks.

Instead of the hospital, I phoned my homeopath, who recommended his friend, an acupuncturist, who twice a week drove up the mountain to treat me on the living room futon. His needles and acupressure massage offered temporary relief to my skin-crawling pain. For a while, my entire stable of health-care givers came to me: the homeopath, the craniosacral therapist, the nurses who showered and dressed me every morning, and of course, Georges, until gradually the inflammation to my nervous system subsided, and I began to rejoin the world outside my apartment.

§

July 1995: Mom visited for a month. Surrounded by old friends, we sat on the patio at two picnic tables pushed together, while the sun slowly sank into the crevice between two peaks. On three sides, mountain ranges: the Vercors, the Belledonne, the Chartreuse. As the lights of the city below began to flicker on, I saw the main boulevards, the twin high-rise apartments, the railroad station.

"This spot is a *coin magique*, a magical spot, Mrs. Seliger," Maria said.

"True, but it's too far away from America. My daughter belongs in her house in Storrs."

"Mom, you've always wanted me close. When Stu and I married, you expected us to move back into my old room instead of renting an apartment."

"That's the European way, isn't it?" She looked to Maria, then Michèle, then Claude.

"Maybe for our parents," Claude answered, "but not for any of us. Have more cantaloupe, Mrs. Seliger. It's sweet and juicy."

§

Mom was a wizard in the kitchen. *Pirogen*, those doughy crescent dumplings filled with potatoes mashed with sautéed onions and farmer cheese, were among her specialties. "I can do anything with potatoes. In Poland that's what you always had."

"Let's make *pirogen* tomorrow. My acupuncturist is coming to give me a treatment. Maybe he could have lunch with us before."

"But we have to get up early. It's a big job. And you have to have all the ingredients."

"Stu will buy them at Satoriz, the organic supermarket. You can go with him this afternoon to pick out the best potatoes."

"Good idea. He's such a quick shopper. He grabs without looking. Spends good money on rotten fruit and vegetables."

"He has too much to do. Because I can't shop alone anymore, that's one more thing on his list."

"You're so lucky to have him. Don't you worry when he's in Connecticut and you're in France, he'll get lonely and find another woman?"

"Mom, how many times have we been through this? I'm here to get cured."

"But you still can't walk. I hate those ski poles and your walker."

Would you like a wheelchair better? I think but don't dare say. Not to Mom, not to me. The MS wasn't supposed to progress. "You have a benign case," my internist said, when, years back I complained at my annual check-up that I had felt unstable negotiating the icy campus the past winter. But what did they know in the eighties? Even today neurologists and researchers still don't know what triggers the immune system to begin attacking itself. Nor have they figured out either how to stop these battles or how to repair the damage. No excuse for a disease diagnosed in 1868 by Dr. Jean Martin Charcot.

"You're in such good condition," Chris said after I'd recovered from my second exacerbation in 1979. "It's too late for me, but I'm sure they'll find a cure in the next five years."

From your mouth to God's ears, I should've said. That's one of Mom's favorite sayings.

§

While Mom boiled five pounds of potatoes in their skins and diced then sautéed a large yellow onion, I sat on the seat of my rolling walker. Several inches higher than my kitchen chairs, it was just the right height for cooking and cleaning up after. My oak mill stood on the counter between stove and sink. Over a foot tall, seven and a quarter inches wide and equally deep, with a three-and-a-half-inch long spout and a removable square lid, every day it ground at least one of my organic grains into flour. "You need live food," my Kousmine dietician said. "After three weeks, ground flour's dead. It lacks nutrients."

I loved the feel of the warm crushed grain between my thumb and index finger, which was how I knew when to tighten or loosen the knob, depending on whether I wanted fine flour or oat flakes. I never tired of watching the flour spill out into my bowl or measuring cup and when neighboring children stopped by, I'd grind wheat berries and let them feel fresh flour.

"Don't mind the noise, Ma. I'm about to turn on my mill. You said eight cups?"

"Yes. In Zurawno I used to go to the mill to get flour for Mama's baking. Sacks full I carried over my shoulder like a peasant. So heavy I came home pale and sweaty. But I was Mama's favorite and whatever she asked, I did."

How many times did Mom tell me how good she was to her mother? how beloved in return? Were these intentional slaps to contrast with my lack of unconditional respect? my sassiness? Or was it Mom's selective way of remembering, which is no different from the way each one of us remembers what may or may not have happened?

Did she need to see herself as Grandma's favorite always helping, unlike her "selfish sisters," in order to silence her guilt for having left her mother (and father) to get married in Belgrade in 1938? for being alive in Brooklyn when they were denounced by their Ukrainian neighbors, tossed into a pit with Zurawno's Jews. "Survivor guilt," Holocaust researchers have named this phenomenon which persecutes the living and often passes down to the second generation. Garland wrote that "Children of . . . survivors have an intense need to act as redeemers for their parents."

That was me, my parents's *naches* machine, always needing to bring them joy, pleasure, gratification, pride. That's why for all those years I hid my MS, trying to protect them from my imperfection, which I feared would be another catastrophe. Only by becoming a writer despite Mom's criticism, then moving to France, the coup de grâce, did I finally separate and become my own Joan. "I don't recognize you anymore," Mom often said. I could've answered, "Nor do I."

§

At noontime my acupuncturist tooted his arrival. In a few minutes he was hugging and kissing me, Stu, and Mom, on both cheeks. I will always miss the warmth of this traditional French greeting. No walls, no distance, just the instinctive crush of two bodies momentarily coming together in friendship.

We sat on the patio, my acupuncturist and I facing the gently sloping Vercors mountain range, while Stu and Mom brought out lunch. "My mother and I spent all morning preparing *pirogen*. It's one of her specialties."

Stu carried out the bowl of homemade yogurt, apple juice, and pitcher of water. Mom followed with a tray-load of magnificent *pirogen* slick with my extra-virgin olive oil, instead of her usual melted butter.

"Look!" she said. "They're black, not white. It's what the peasants ate in Poland." Her face wrinkled in anger.

"That's because I ground whole wheat berries. This flour's alive, not dead like the processed flour you buy in the supermarket."

"I don't care. All morning we worked, and for what?"

"Sit down and eat, Ma. I'm sure they're delicious."

"Yes, Mrs. Seliger. It's delicious," my acupuncturist said, after a few bites.

But watching Mom sulk over the one *pirog* she tasted put a damper on our lunch.

"*Quel monstre!*" my acupuncturist said, as he pressed to find the tender spots, then carefully placed his disposable needles along my spine. We'd escaped to the privacy of my bedroom. That afternoon he worked for a long time getting the needles to release my body's stress and let energy flow.

§

Although she was almost eighty-five, despite her recent battle with Hodgkin's disease, as well as a broken hip, Mom had the appearance and vitality of someone at least ten years younger. In Delray Beach, without a cane she walked to the clubhouse pool and swam every day, entertaining her circle of widows with stories of her childhood in Zurawno, Poland, or her three-month escape from Hitler, which included crossing the Tigris on a mule, resting on a rock while a peasant tested the river.

Since Dad's death in 1987, Mom has found her voice. Not that she was timid, but in public she let him take center stage, as if her memories meant less. These days, however, she is unstoppable, making it her mission to tell everyone she meets, including my friends, that she will never forgive the Nazis.

"But Ma, even Elie Wiesel, who was in Auschwitz says, 'Forgive but don't forget.'"

"I don't care what Elie Wiesel says."

We argue in circles with me struggling to separate myself from Mom's other mostly critical viewpoints—including the grudges she's held since childhood when one sister or another "wouldn't mop the kitchen floor unless I held the bucket"— as well as her ongoing negativity. I try to teach her the lesson I've been learning at l'Arche about forgiveness: You forgive the person, not the deed. Otherwise you carry the anger/hatred/grievance in your heart, leaving less room for love.

But after all her losses, what right do I have to chastise Mom, or at her age, to force on her what I've chosen to learn?

Nonetheless, each day of her Venon visit, we attacked and parried over every difference of opinion: two equally stubborn women. Mom insisted she knew best, defending her most outrageous ideas by quipping: "My friends in Florida tell me once you pass eighty, you can say anything and you're always right!"

Although she has said this so many times that it's a family joke, why do I keep contradicting her? Am I less trainable than a laboratory rat, who after a few electric shocks learns to avoid pathways that cause pain?

Six years later back in Storrs, my Yan Xin Qigong® group will tell me to welcome everyone you meet as your teacher, to ask yourself: Why does she or he tick me off? What is she or he mirroring that I need to change in my own behavior in order to become a better person? But back then, I too, wanted my way and couldn't let go of either the large or "small stuff." Nor did I understand that although Mom's physical condition made me envious—if only I could walk the mountain roads as she did, instead of sitting in my Quickie wheelchair, relying on someone to push—something was attacking her brain cells, stealing her short-term memory as well as her ability to think rationally.

The day before Stu flew to Newcastle for a conference, Mom and I were sitting on the balcony drinking tea.

"We'll have to pack today for our five days at the abbey."

"Why can't we stay here?" she asked, as if a few hours ago I hadn't told her about Stu's impending trip.

"Because when Stu's in England, he won't be able to drive us anywhere."

"You used to drive. Why don't you drive again?"

Was she blind or was she making fun of me? Didn't she see that even with the rolling walker I could barely get my legs to take me room to room?

"How many times have I told you, I haven't been able to drive since the attack? Don't you see I can't even go up and down the stairs without Stu taking me in the wheelchair?"

"Oh, I haven't noticed. If you're getting worse, you should come home."

"What do you want from me?" I shrieked. "Can't you leave me in peace, you monster? I hate you!" tumbled out of my mouth for the first time in my life, catapulting me and Mom into hysterics. Stu put his arms around me, pulling me close, while Colette miraculously appeared to hug Mom and lead her away.

§

The next morning Stu drove us to l'Arche. On the left side of the autoroute, we rode alongside the Vercors mountain range, glacier-sculpted to domes and mesas, with arguably the best cross-country trails in France. It was here in spring '72, after Larry, my third son's birth—our only Frenchman—that I learned to jog from one of Stu's colleagues, Jean-Paul, a double-marathon champion, nationally, in his middle-age category. "Double-breathe: in-in, out-out," he'd chant, his finger poking my back, ultimately coaxing me through the forest and up and down the steep trails, until the rest of his Friday afternoon group and I would collapse over a *tarte aux fruits* and *infusion* at a local café. And it was in these mountains, winter '78–'79, that Jean-Paul and his *équipe* taught me to duck-walk up a cross-country slope, so I wouldn't keep slipping down.

Stu parked outside the kitchen entrance avoiding stairs, then wheeled me to the office where Jeannette welcomed each of us with a kiss on both cheeks. Those who call the French cold, distant, hostile to foreigners, must be the tourists who frequent hotels and order *"grapefruit"* from the waiters, not the lucky ones like me who've spent years living in a typical French village, embraced by everyone as their most honored guest.

Jeannette gave us a large, airy room adjacent to the unisex bathroom, which houses four stalls and a sink with cold water. Mom closed the door. "I don't want to stay. We don't belong here."

"Why not?"

"We're the only Jews. I saw that woman's cross. Those people we passed in the kitchen had them, too."

"Calm down, Ma. That wooden cross indicates they're members of this community. I'm taking the calligraphy workshop. There's even an Israeli folk-dance workshop, so there are bound to be some Jews."

"If you say so." She looked around at the two beds separated by night tables, then opened the closet of shelves and unpacked our suitcases. "The beds look comfortable. I'm ready for a nap."

"Me, too. But first I need a kiss." I wheeled over to Mom, stretched out my arms and gently pulled her toward me, feeling the softness of her cheek against my lips. It smelled lightly of the Oil of Olay she smoothed on her face and neck, morning and night.

"Your friend Colette is so affectionate. Every time she sees me, she hugs and kisses me." That's Colette, I thought, wishing I could open my heart so readily.

I was grateful to Colette for mothering Mom yesterday. "How did you calm her?" I asked before leaving.

"Like this." She opened her strong arms and held me tight, massaging the tension out of my back and shoulders. Then I told her, 'Joan is very sick. She needs you to see that. To love her anyway.'"

"I always love her, even when she makes me cry. She's my only daughter."

"Go with her to the abbey, Mrs. Seliger. She needs you to do that."

§

Fall semester: Jean Derioz, the English Department Head at l'Université de Grenoble III (Stendhal: Langues et Lettres), has hired me full-time as a *maître de langue étrangère*—master of foreign language—to start a creative writing program on the heels of last fall's successful mini-elective. Although passing me in the hall, he saw me in my Quickie wheel-chair with Stu or my taxi driver pushing, he never asked what happened to my rolling walker, nor did I volunteer. He has blessed me with a lighter load than my colleagues: three two-hour classes, including English conver-sation in a high-tech language lab, plus recording at home for a blind stu-dent one hour of current events from the *International Herald Tribune*.

Although I had never been happier professionally, my body refused to play along. At home, in between doses of Chinese pills, the spasms left me screeching and crying until my voice became a croak. On the other side of the wall, Colette listened as helpless as I was to soothe the pain. At the same time, despite e-mail postings as far away as Lyon, Stu couldn't find a mathematician to job-swap second semester; nor, with winter coming, could we find a first-floor apartment in Venon.

"When the stairs are icy," my taxi-driver said, "I can't carry you in your wheelchair up and down."

By the time our youngest son, Larry, arrived for Christmas break, his suitcase packed with the L.L. Bean winter slacks and sweaters I'd ordered, our decision had made itself. But how could I tell Jean who had done everything to give me this opportunity?

Larry drove me down to campus, wheeling me to the language lab.

Our discussion subject that day was a feminist article on sex-role stereo-types: Larry and the lone male student who showed up that afternoon versus fourteen vocal females. At the end, as everyone raced out the door, my left leg spasmed, jamming my foot under the desk. I yelled and he extricated me. That night I phoned Jean.

§

Winter 1996, Storrs, Connecticut: No matter how familiar I thought I was with the American medical system, especially as it contrasted with the socialized medicine of France, I was unprepared for its gifts. My friend whose home health agency staff cares for Chris insisted I phone her consulting MS neurologist to replace my doctor who just weeks before had left Yale. Within days, a Belgian-born neurologist, attractive enough to be on the cover of *Vogue*, showed up at my door to give me a complete examination and ordered an at-home IV Solumedrol series of treatments—a daily high-dose cortisone drip for five days—which entitled me to months of home health aides, who unpacked and helped me settle back into my house.

Taking the cortisone-based drug was my trade-off. After thirty years of refusing allopathic drugs, I was ready to try almost anything to free me from my prison of pain. For the first time, I understood those who committed suicide with Dr. Kevorkian or other compassionate helpers. When pain steals every second of one's life, leaving no room for love or joy, how dare we judge? I looked at my bottle of a hundred Chinese pills, comforted by their presence.

Within a few weeks, however, the Solumedrol wore off, and the relentless pain and spasticity in my legs returned. I wound up in the office of a physiatrist, a specialist in rehabilitative medicine. He prescribed Neurontin, a new muscle relaxer, and proposed surgically implanting an intrathecal Baclofen pump, which would automatically release miniscule doses of Baclofen, another muscle relaxer, directly into my nervous system.

Although desperate, I was not ready for spinal surgery or living with a medical device that might require maintenance or replacement. The Joan that thrives on life abroad didn't need to be tied in place by technology.

Instead I opted for oral therapy, first trying Zanaflex, a newly FDA-approved muscle relaxer that, while calming my pain, shot my liver functions to ten times above normal, but made me realize that if relatively pain-free, I could function while on high doses of medications. Immediately, the neurologist switched me to Baclofen. As the dosage built, the pain and spasms diminished, and I returned to everyday life.

To the Baclofen my neurologist added Copaxone. "Instead of your immune system attacking itself, your t-cells will attack the drug."

In the beginning, Stu mixed the two vials, transferred them to a syringe and injected. "Finally I'm a Jewish doctor. Grandma would have been proud." But with the new format of prefilled syringes, all I have to do is self-inject.

§

What is everyday life? Most weekday mornings instead of starting with breakfast, Stu dresses me in my bathing suit. It's a tug of war as I sit on our handicapped toilet seat, twenty inches from the floor, then grab the heavy-duty stainless-steel bars bolted to the bathroom walls and hoist my body high enough for Stu to pull up the suit over my buttocks. "One, two, three, go," I say, as he struggles. "You're not high enough, your butt is barely off the seat." Sometimes it takes as many as five tries until the suit is straight and I slip my breasts into the bra cups. Next I pull on a turtle-neck or tee-shirt, depending on the season, then he pulls up my slacks or shorts, saving me energy and several minutes. Instead of shoes, I wear socks and bootie-type slippers or go barefoot in summer.

Who drives the five minutes to the UConn pool depends on whether there's open space for me to automatically lock behind the steering wheel, after driving up the ramp of our handicapped-accessible Windstar, or whether Stu's seat's locked in the driving position. Fortunately, with muscle power and sweat, he can unlock, then shift his seat to the passenger side, giving us both independence.

My counselors at the Bureau of Rehabilitation Services (BRS), their colleague who authorizes vehicle modifications, and the Handicapped Division of the Department of Motor Vehicles (DMV) put me back in the driver's seat. A slow, bureaucratic process, it took a year before we saw the ramped van with its lowered floor and middle seats removed, among many other modifications. For all that time, either Stu or an occasional friend would take me to appointments, including writing workshops I gave at local high schools, the Center for Learning in Retirement, or the weekly "Writing for Your Life" adult workshop I began teaching for my town.

Even weighing in at only ninety-two pounds, it's not easy to transfer me from a car to my Quickie manual chair, which Stu managed with only an occasional bump to my elbow or head. When my women friends chauffeured me, I wouldn't hesitate to flag down an extra pair of arms. As Chris told me years back, "Most people want to help. They just have to be told how." "No, I can't," is another acceptable response, I've learned. Not to take it personally. Maybe it's an issue that he or she is working out or simply a physical problem, which has nothing to do with me. But I'm no longer afraid to ask.

My Windstar and my motorized wheelchair arrived within a month of each other. The latter, a Permobil from Sweden, was "the Cadillac of wheelchairs," the sales rep claimed. "It turns on a dime. Outside at high speed you could outrace your husband when he's walking." But he neglected to tell me it would take weeks of patience and practice to master, just as learning to drive the van would require.

When I crashed my footrests through the back wall of my study in an attempt to zigzag to the toilet, I called him to complain. "You sold me the wrong chair. It's much too unwieldy for the tight corners of my house."

Somehow my physical therapist convinced insurance to have her teach me. "They've invested $20,000 in your chair. It makes sense that they'd pay a little more to have you learn to use it." An expert teacher as well as PT, in no time this smiling, no-nonsense woman taught me to negotiate my entire first floor. In the months that followed, it was Stu and our visiting adult children who scraped the pine floors and chiseled the wood trim.

Finally comfortable with the Permobil, I could begin driving lessons from the wheelchair. Used to driving station wagons and sedans, and not having driven for a year and a half, I wondered what the van would feel like. One early afternoon by appointment, a husky, six-foot-three man in a blue suit showed up to take me on the road. But first he walked me through everything up front, especially the hand controls.

"Push the handle on your left out straight. That's your brake. Push it down and it's your gas."

Before starting the engine, I tried it several times. Pushing the handle felt awkward, but I liked the panoramic view from the van.

"Now start the car. I want you to drive very slowly down your driveway. Begin braking halfway down. Both gas and brake are extra sensitive."

I inched halfway down, then touched the brake. "Sorry," as we stopped short. "Good time for seat belts."

"It's always a good time for seat belts. Told you those brakes were sensitive." He was smiling. "Take the car a little further, then try to brake more gently."

Did it take us an hour to go the mile around my neighborhood circle, or did time reflect my growing frustration? He kept having me go a few yards, then start to brake. I felt as if I were riding a bucking bronco. "It's much harder than I thought. Will I ever be able to do it?" I asked when we were safely parked in front of my garage.

"I've been training handicapped drivers for over thirty years. Let's try again next week."

§

Fall 2003: Although I drive locally without hesitation, twenty minutes has been my usual limit. It's either Stu or a close friend who takes me to long-distance medical appointments. "Don't push yourself," my doctors have said. "You have nothing to prove." I know, but I long for those days I took for granted.

Despite the many medicines to control my pain and spasticity, which I'm sure contribute to my almost daily need to nap, most days I'm off and running: swimming, PT or other medical, academic, or social appointments. "You do more than any healthy person I know," my homeopath (both an MD and a DHt) said recently. It was not a compliment. "You have to choose."

But I don't know how. "Joanie, you want to swallow the world," my mother used to say.

"Ask God to help you," my very devout physical therapists at Crossroads say. "You're His chosen people. When the Jews were slaves in Egypt and stressed, what did they do? Pray."

I try not to think of the Holocaust, blaming God for abandoning six million Jews (plus millions of others, including gypsies, homosexuals, and anyone caught helping Jews). Instead I reframe: Because God gave us free will to do both good and evil, He/She couldn't intervene. How He/She must suffer along with the oppressed, watching over and over as we destroy ourselves and our environment!

§

March 2004: My homeopath and I have been working together to help me understand why my body has been going through two months of intermittent diarrhea, a pattern which started in France when I was super stressed. Not convenient to feel a twinge in my abdomen and have my bowels let go almost instantaneously.

"Tell me about the twinge," he said.

"It's a slight tightening, a momentary sharp warning signal that propels me to the toilet."

"And your abdomen?"

"Knotted. As if lots of hands are tying thick, rough twine in big knots up and down and across my abdomen. I feel like the hands are all the issues I'm dealing with. They pull tight, making me a prisoner. I feel bloated, resentment in my body, helpless, angry." I reach for a tissue.

"What's the connection between stress and diarrhea?"

"All I need is a phone call from one of my adult children telling me about a health problem or an injustice at work. I hang up, run to the toilet and empty out. Or in my own life. I keep hitting concrete walls."

I tell him about our "too good to be true" Florida vacation, a pre-Christmas trip that turned out to be an internet scam. The days spent preparing a complaint to the Florida Department of Consumer Protection to prevent others from falling victim, which went nowhere. And my ongoing battles as a handicapped advocate, constantly fighting for access instead of exclusion.

He pulls a book by Vermuelen off the shelf of his eclectic library and begins to read to me about a remedy called Staphysagria. "Heroes and knights . . . knotted sensation internally."

"It strikes me you're idealistic, jousting with much larger forces, injustice like Don Quixote. But you don't have his element of foolishness. You don't tilt at windmills. You have diarrhea in response to these social, emotional situations.

"We want to see this as a good thing, that your body defends. But in a way that's costly. The goal is to have normal bms and not to have diarrhea in these situations.

"Illness is a consequence of the unattunement, not walking the path. My job as a homeopath is to bring the organism into tune so you can walk the path. Craft meaning out of life."

He folds a piece of paper, origami-like, into a container; pours a stream of Staphysagria pellets in and flicks a few onto my tongue. The rest he pours into a tiny brown vial. "Take them once a day for a week, then call."

§

For the first time in public, when I was on the physical therapist's table as she stretched my legs, my bowels let go—"No biggie," she said, then helped me clean up with baby wipes. "For protection," she put on a diaper, then dressed me in a pair of jeans she'd found in the closet. "A perfect fit."

What did it feel like at age sixty-one to be in a diaper? No biggie, as she said, secure as I drove home. Happily there were no more public accidents, but it was time to change remedies. And we did.

Mid-May, 2004: "Better but not where it should be," my homeopath says.

"According to my PTs, I'm constantly in fight or flight mode. Stress hits my gut and it turns to fluid. My bowel movements are foul like a cesspool."

"What was your life like before MS?"

I tell him I hiked and downhill-skied a little. With an outing club, I rushed to the top of a mountain, wanting to be first; to stand and survey the labyrinthine paths below, the forests, the panorama. This was God's country. I was with like-minded people. Nothing was missing.

"Does anything else give you that feeling?"

"When I'm writing." I reach for a tissue. "Before I got lost in poems, now in memoir. I get pissed if Stuart dares to come into my study, even to get the stapler. I don't want reality. I'm in a faraway place, deep inside me. So fulfilling."

"I'd like to try Falcon peregrinus. The falcon is a prisoner in the mountains, blindfolded and tied with ropes. Your stool symptoms fit, too: loose, explosive, slight pains, out of control."

§

Two days later Stu and I escape for a week's vacation in the Berkshires, a two-and-a-half-hour drive from Storrs. Our timeshare exchange (our newest venture) is partway up the road to Jiminy Peak. On both sides, the oaks and maples have leafed out. We are engulfed in green.

The unit itself is handicapped-accessible, as promised. There are cutouts by the stove, kitchen and bathroom sinks, so I can roll under easily. The shower is roll-in with a bench. The toilet seat is raised but the transfer bars, though Americans with Disabilities Act (ADA) compliant—one size fits all—are out of my reach. Only at home from my customized toilet can I transfer independently. Same problem with the unit's king-size bed. No trapeze for me to grab and pull myself up to sitting. Some vacation for Stu, who winds up doing all my transfers! Despite arthritis in his left knee and hip, he's become the master of bending at the knees, reaching under my arms and pivoting me to and fro.

"Let's drive up to Mt. Greylock," I say one afternoon. "It's practically next door." Mt. Greylock at 3,491 feet is the highest spot in Massachusetts.

There's a wheelchair-accessible path from the parking lot to the vista, a panorama of trails and trees that makes my heart beat faster. While Stu climbs the monument, I breathe in the view.

"Let's see where this gravel path leads." I turn left and he follows. "Look, it's the Appalachian Trail!" Was 1982 after the Aspen Writers Conference, my first writers' conference, the last time my feet touched that trail? I had come home strong from two weeks of hiking around Maroon Bells, and to the Continental Divide, after writing workshops. We were spending two weeks at Plumley House in Vermont. Access to the Appalachian Trail, which wends from Maine to Georgia, was only a few miles away, so I prepared peanut butter and jelly sandwiches and led the six of us into the woods.

"Stu, please get the camera. I want a picture of me next to this Appalachian Trail sign."

"But don't go any further. I don't want you getting stuck."

Ignoring his words, I turned onto the trail. Immediately my left wheel spun uselessly in the dirt beyond the gravel. The more I tried to go forward or back, the deeper the hole I dug.

"Why couldn't you listen?"

"Please help us," I asked the sturdy-looking woman about to enter the trail.

She pulled while Stu pushed. In a minute I was free.

"Thanks a lot." She smiled and walked on.

"I caught my finger," Stu said. "I'm going to the lodge to wash and bandage it."

It looked like a superficial cut but I could tell he was fed up with me. He hadn't understood my joy at being on the Appalachian Trail, its symbolic past, which he had barely shared.

At the lodge a young woman working there asked him, "Do you teach Math. at UConn?"

"Yes."

"Professor Sidney, I had you for first-year calculus in 1999."

Though he couldn't remember her name or face, she saved the day.

The next evening we met a friend for dinner. Her carrot out-of-control curls were tinged with gray. How many years since she slept over and we did yoga postures on my Oriental rug? She'd been part of my foursome at the New Jersey Writing Project, July '81. Each weekday morning we wrote, then divided into our assigned groups and read. After a few days of boring academic writing, I reworked the poems I'd slid out of their hiding place. "We want more," my audience agreed. "That's your passion, not the academic jargon." To please them and myself, I began to write poetry.

After listening to the details of my aborted hike, she looked at me and laughed. "You've always been the adventurous one. But you still need Stu to get you out of trouble."

"No, that's only half true," Stu said. "Joanie also needs me to get her into trouble."

§

Saturday, May 22, our last morning of vacation: eight a.m. and as usual we open the indoor pool. Unlike most hotel pools, more like places to splash than lap swim, this pool is seventy-five feet long. There's room for Stu to swim twice as fast and not drown me in his wake. With walls of windows in front and to the right of the room, the mountains feel almost poolside. As I do my usual routine: breaststroke up, crawl back—both with the flutter kick since my legs still won't spread into a frog or whip kick—the sun pokes through the clouds. My arms stroke through a trail of sparkling light.

ACKNOWLEDGMENTS

These poems first appeared, sometimes in earlier versions, in the following publications, to whose editors grateful acknowledgment is made:

Atlantis (Canada): "Forging Links" (as "At Birkenau"); *Connecticut River Review*: "Leaving," "*Oysgevept*," "Witness";" *Exquisite Reaction*: "Venon, France"; *Fall Down 7 Times, Get Up 8*: "Jin Shin Do"; *Israel Horizons*: "Family History"; *Jewish Currents*: "Ache," "Malka at Ninety"; *Kaimana*: "Next Door" (as "Houses Down the Road"); *Louisville Review*: "Betrayal"; *Michigan Quarterly Review*: "Laps," "Poker"; *Midstream*: "For the New Year"; *Moments in Time* (France): "Castoffs," "The Sunday News"; *My Glass is Cracked: Poems by Poets Whose Glass is Neither Half-Full Nor Half-Empty*: "Stamps"; *Potpourri*: "Vespers"; *Sing Heavenly Muse!*: "Naming"; *Massachusetts Review*: "Preserves"; *New York Quarterly*: "Naming," "Poker" (as "Games"); *Urim V'Tumim*: "One Summer in Connecticut"; *Writing Women* (England): "Nude" (as "The Exhibitionist"); *Yellow Silk*: "Coming Home"; *Yuan Yang* (Hong Kong): "Morning Swim."

These poems have been reprinted or are forthcoming in the following publications:

Anthology of Magazine Verse & Yearbook of American Poetry, 1986-88: "For the New Year"; *Beyond Lament: Poets of the World Bearing Witness to the Holocaust*: "Forging Links"; *Bubbe Meisehs by Shayna Maideles*: "For the New Year"; *Cheney Hall Broadside Poetry, 2000-2001*: "Forging Links"; *Her Face in the Mirror: Jewish Women on Mothers and Daughters*: "Poker," "Preserves"; *I Refused to Die: Stories of Boston-area Holocaust Survivors and Liberating World War II Soldiers*: "Belgium, 1942," "For the New Year," "Forging Links"; *Kaleidoscope*: "Jin Shin Do," "Naming," "Preserves," "Stamps," "Venon, France"; *Midstream*: "Belgium, 1942"; *Moments in Time* (France): "Poker"; *Points of Contact: Disability, Art, and*

Culture: "Laps"; *Range of Motion*: "Naming."

Deep Between the Rocks (Andrew Mountain Press, 1985): "Coming Home," "For the New Year," "Belgium, 1942"; *The Way the Past Comes Back* (The Kutenai Press, 1991): "Forging Links," "One Summer in Connecticut," "Poker," "Preserves."

"Vespers" and "Malka at Ninety" were nominated for a Pushcart Prize in 2003. "Vespers" was selected for "Poetic Journeys," then designed and printed as an illustrated broadside to ride the University of Connecticut shuttle buses, December 2001-January 2002. It was reprinted as the December poem in the Poetic Journeys 2004 calendar. "Body of Diminishing Motion" won first prize in the Windham Area Poetry Project (WAPP)'s 2001 contest; "Witness" and "Visit with the Dead" won first prizes in WAPP's 2000 contest; "Flamenco Night at Centre Cap Pèrefite" (as "Rehabilitation") won first prize in WAPP's 1999 contest, "Retreat" an honorable mention; "Laps" and "Betrayal" won first prizes in WAPP's 1998 contest. "Witness" won an honorable mention in the Rockford (IL) Art Museum's 1997 poetry contest.

Excerpts from "Hiking Remote Trails" were published in *Journal of Clinical Epidemiology*: "When there's 'no cure,'" and in *Coping Outlets*: "Healing Stories."

The epigraph by Adrienne Rich: These lines come from Poem 18 of "Contradictions: Tracking Poems." Copyright © 2002, 1986 by Adrienne Rich, from *The Fact of a Doorframe: Selected Poems, 1950-2001* by Adrienne Rich. Used by permission of the author and W. W. Norton & Company, Inc.

The quote by Dorothea Lange is from *Dorothea Lange: A Visual Life*, published by the Smithsonian Institution Press, Washington D.C.; copyright ©

ACKNOWLEDGEMENTS

1994 by Elizabeth Partridge. Used by permission of the Smithsonian Institution Press.

The quote by Susan Sontag is from *Illness as Metaphor*, published by Farrar, Straus & Giroux, copyright © 1978. Used by permission from Farrar, Straus & Giroux.

Thank you to the Connecticut Commission on the Arts for a 2003 poetry grant; the Christopher Reeve Paralysis Foundation for a full fellowship to the Vermont Studio Center (VSC) in 2002; to the VSC for writing fellowships in 1990, 1992, 1998, and 2000; also to Mark Doty, Musa Mayer, and Sharon Doubiago for their critical reading of my manuscript at the VSC; to Ann Mathewson and the University of Connecticut AAUP Professional Development Fund; to Anne Greene, Lisa Reisman, and Craig Arnold of the Wesleyan Writers Conference, 2002; to the Connecticut Bureau of Rehabilitation Services, especially Lelia Hay and LaWanda Cook, for my computers and printers; to the Fortunoff Video Archive for Holocaust Testimonies at Yale University and Eastern Connecticut State University for a Visiting Faculty Fellowship in 1984-5; to Arnold Dashefsky, Lorri Lafontaine, Dianne Tillman, and the University of Connecticut Center for Judaic Studies and Contemporary Jewish Life; to all my teachers and writing groups, especially Joan Joffe Hall, my earliest supporter; to my colleagues Regina Barecca, Lynn Z. Bloom, Jonathan Hufstader, and Penelope Pelizzon. I remain most grateful to Gray Jacobik, Richard Telford, Brad Davis, and my bottom-line critic Robert Cording, whose extraordinary generosity and astute reading have helped my writing evolve. Thanks, too, to CavanKerry Press: to Joan Cusack Handler and Baron Wormser for their editorial insights, and to Peter Cusack and Florenz Greenberg. Lastly, much appreciation to Dan for critiquing my poems, to Stu for his patient reading of seemingly endless drafts, and to all my family for much love and inspiration.